CRITICAL THINKING SKILLS JOURNAL

The Prentice Hall Guide
for College Writers

SIXTH EDITION

Stephen Reid ♦ Christina Murphy

Prentice
Hall

Upper Saddle River, New Jersey 07458

© 2003 by PEARSON EDUCATION, INC.
Upper Saddle River, New Jersey 07458

ISBN 0-13-099301-8

Printed in the United States of America

CONTENTS

PREFACE

This critical thinking journal is designed to encourage writers to think critically about their textbook, the essays they read, the essays they write, and the writing process itself. Critical thinking requires, first of all, that there are differences of belief, judgment, or perception about important ideas. From these differences of point of view come dialogue, discussion, analysis, controversy, and synthesis. The importance of critical thinking lies partly in the dialogue or discussion or rethinking itself, and partly in the fact that a clearer, more accurate perception of the truth emerges from the critical activity.

The following quotation from journalist Walter Lippmann (which appears on the first page of Chapter Ten) stresses the importance of debate and critical thinking:

> Freedom of speech is established to achieve
> its essential purpose only when different
> opinions are expounded in the same hall
> to the same audience. . . .
> The opposition is indispensable.

Lippmann is arguing for the belief that <u>controversy</u>, <u>dialogue</u>, and <u>debate</u> are essential to our freedoms. Critical thinking is a basic skill that enables us to articulate and then counter opposing or alternative arguments. Critical thinking is a mental rehearsal, if you will, for those public conversations, dialogues, and debates that we enter when we write down our ideas for others. Critical thinking encourages us not to accept the status quo, but to anticipate other points of view, and in the process, clarify our thinking and bring us closer to understanding the complexity of truth. A critical thinking journal allows writers to generate and record key arguments on ideas relevant to the writing process.

Critical thinking is at the heart of the academic writing students do at a college or university, but it is equally important for careers after students graduate. In college, writers are frequently asked, during class discussions and on essay responses, to explain, create, analyze, judge, debate, and reflect on important course concepts. In real life jobs, too, employees often work in teams, analyzing problems, discussing possible solutions, and considering alternative plans. In an essay entitled, "On Planning a Career,"

Robert B. Reich, a professor of political economy at Harvard University, explains to his students the importance of critical thinking in preparing for change:

> The courses to which you now gravitate may be helpful to understand how a particular job is <u>now</u> done, but irrelevant to how such a job <u>will</u> be done. The intellectual equipment needed for the job of the future is an ability to define problems, quickly assimilate relevant data . . . reorganize the information . . . ask hard questions about it, discuss findings with colleagues, work collaboratively to find solutions, and then convince others.

This critical thinking journal, in conjunction with the text, prepares writers to challenge comfortable assumptions, to ask the hard questions as they solve the problems in reading, writing, and thinking that they face in a college writing course.

TO THE STUDENT:
USING THE CRITICAL THINKING JOURNAL

The major premise of this critical thinking journal is that <u>writing down</u> your thoughts and ideas--rather than just thinking to yourself--aids in the writing process. In an actual essay, you cannot just think about what you would like to say; you must actually write something down. The difference between thinking about something in your head and actually committing your ideas to paper is like the difference between thinking out a tennis match and actually playing one. <u>Only by learning to think with your pen moving can you practice the skills you need to write well</u>. So the first rule of this journal is never just think, "Oh, I know what I'd say in answer to that question." Instead, write down your thoughts. Often, you'll surprise yourself with what you think when you begin to put words on paper.

The second rule of this journal is that there is not a specific answer you must give to each question. In fact, you probably don't want to methodically answer every question asked. Each of the exercises that follows contains a set of interrelated questions designed to set you thinking and writing about a particular topic or writing assignment. As you respond in writing to these questions, react to the questions as a whole, rather than answering each question individually. At first, you may have a tendency to want to answer each question individually, as though your critical thinking journal were a sort of fill-in-the-blanks workbook. Nothing could be farther from the purpose of this journal. Instead, <u>use the questions to begin your own creative thinking about the topic,</u> and then express in writing the ideas that have come to your mind.

The third rule for writing in this journal is be patient. Be willing to listen for your own voice, your own ideas, and your own reactions. <u>When you come up with one of your own ideas, be willing to explore that and see where your idea leads</u>. Think of each writing assignment as an intellectual problem, a creative challenge to your thinking skills. And then be willing to trust your own ideas, not what you think is necessarily the right answer. Confidence in writing comes slowly, so you must be willing to listen for your own voice and your own ideas, and then shape those ideas in words. The patience and confidence you gain answering the questions in this journal will pay off when you're writing your way through an important essay assignment for this course.

Most writers believe that they start writing when they sit down with their pen or pencil, or when they sit at their computer or typewriter. The fact is, however, that most writing begins with a writing situation: a **writer** who wishes or needs to **inform** or **persuade** or have some particular effect on a **reader** or readers. Even before writers sort through which letters and symbols they need, they begin with a writing situation, a context for needing or wanting to write.

Chapter One: Myths and Rituals

Here is everything you need for writing well:

abcdefghijklmnopqrstuvwxyz

1234567890

! ? , ; : . " ' ( ) / [ ]

Well, actually, there is one thing missing. You. Or, more precisely, your imagination and creativity, for one truth of the writing process is that each writer begins with the same twenty-six letters, the same nine digits, and the same handful of punctuation marks. The only thing that separates one writer from the next is the way that he or she chooses to put these letters, these numbers, these punctuation marks together in order to create meaningful statements to share with others.

No one can say exactly how your imaginative, creative process will work; no one can know precisely the ideas your mind will formulate. All that can be said is that the ideas you develop will be unique, the result of your own particular experience of the world. Therefore, your creative process should be a source of wonder and fascination for you, and learning to understand your own thinking processes should enable you to think with even greater depth and clarity. Here are some ideas associated with the concept of thinking: to form an idea in the mind; to have a thought; to reason about, reflect upon, or ponder; to decide; to judge or regard; to believe or suppose; to expect, anticipate, or hope; to remember, call to mind, or imagine; to visualize; to exercise the power of reason; to draw inferences and make judgments; to weigh something carefully; to contemplate.

All ideas about thinking and the mind reveal how complex and unique each person's consciousness is as the source of all intellectual creativity. The chances are, though, that if you are like most people, you haven't given a great deal of thought to your own thinking and creative processes--at least enough thought to figure out if there is a pattern to your thinking and if that pattern can be improved upon and enhanced. The question of how thinking and creativity work in the writing process is thus a perfect focus for your initial entries in your critical thinking journal.

1

Exercise #1

The following statements express common myths or misperceptions about writing. Read these statements and, on the following page, explain a probable <u>source</u> for several of these myths. (In some cases, the speaker is simply insecure about writing, while in other cases, the speaker may be misinformed about the writing or the real world.) Try to find one myth you agree with and explain your position.

• "Writing is something you either can do or you can't. People who can write are born with it."

• "Writing is not an important skill in today's world anymore. We have other means of communicating with each other, like telephones and TV."

• "If you make any changes in your first draft, you'll ruin your creativity."

• "When I get my first job, I won't need to write because I'll have a secretary who'll do it for me."

• "An essay will only be good if you make an outline first."

• "Freshman English is only required because nobody would take it if they didn't have to."

• "All good essays must have an introduction, three paragraphs, and a conclusion."

• "Pretty soon they'll have computers that will fix everything for you in writing, so I don't have to learn all that unimportant, boring grammar stuff."

Freewriting

This critical thinking journal will often ask for you to freewrite on a variety of issues and topics.

Although freewriting may seem to be busy work--after all, you're using time that you could spend actually writing your next assignment or doing your chemistry--it has several clear <u>benefits</u> for you. First, freewriting is a good place to <u>warm up</u>, physically and mentally, to get your thoughts and ideas flowing before you start writing a specific assignment. Next, researchers have shown that by writing frequently and regularly, you become more comfortable with putting your thoughts down on paper and your <u>overall fluency</u> improves. Third, freewriting helps you <u>overcome writer's block</u> caused by trying to write out a "final version" of your ideas as you put pencil to paper. If you realize that your first thoughts can be ungraded, rambling passages that have sentence or spelling errors, you increase your ability to concentrate on what you're saying and forget, for a moment, how your writing should look. A final value of freewriting is that it allows you to develop your unique ideas and associations about topics and ideas. Good writing always has an element of <u>discovery or surprise,</u> and freewriting gives you a chance to discover what your ideas are and surprise yourself!

When you begin freewriting, do just what it says. Fix your mind on a subject and write nonstop for a period of time. Write freely--that is, do not worry about grammar, punctuation, spelling, etc.--and do not go back and change what you have written. If your mind wanders or your focus shifts, do not interrupt the flow of your ideas or fight the new direction that is developing. You might discover some of your best ideas by letting your mind and your creative processes shape the flow of your ideas, even if, at the time, the direction your ideas move might seem odd or insignificant to you. A good piece of advice is **follow the flow**.

The most important goal of freewriting is to get over your fear that you have nothing to say. You have begun writing, and you can look at the pages you write and see your mind at work. In addition, freewriting allows for other opportunities for writing so that, once you have completed a freewriting entry, you can isolate particular ideas from the first entry and use them as starting points for other freewritings. Often, repeated freewritings become topics that you can write about for your instructor. Even if they are not your final topics, however, your freewriting gives you practice in developing your ideas through several impromptu and informal drafts.

Here is a sample freewriting on the topic of "Dieting" that indicates how this process might work.

. . . .

No more chocolate cake. 6:00 A.M. walks or jogs. Cottage cheese and melba toast. Oh my God! I can't do this. All my life I've been over-weight. Why do I have to change now? Sorority rush coming. Dates and evening dresses. I'll look like a blimp. That's even if I get asked at all. I wish I didn't like food so much. Mom's casseroles are what did this to me. If she wasn't such a good cook, I wouldn't have eaten so much. Wrong. There's always McDonald's. And Pizza Hut. Not to mention the refrigerator. Why am I always so eager to blame someone else for my problem? Maybe I could learn to love green beans. A green bean milk shake. YUCK! A green bean pizza. Getting worse. Maybe a little discipline with what I do eat. Like maybe one sandwich instead of two. Like maybe skipping that afternoon candy bar and Coke. Like maybe eating for my health rather than for my entertainment and pleasure. Like maybe thinking of dieting as a good thing and not as a punishment. Like maybe knowing if I dieted right once and stuck to it I might never have to diet again. Ever.

. . . .

Now consider what this student did by isolating a topic from her first freewriting and generating freewriting #2.

. . . .

Why do I always blame someone else for my weight problem? Like Mom? Like my bone structure? Like genetics, like fate, like God? Because it's easier and less painful. When I step into the dressing room and I've gone up still another size, I don't have to look in the mirror and say, "Why can't you love yourself enough to have some self-control? Why do you use food for your source of fun and comfort instead of friends and activities? Why do you feel such a need to punish yourself and to fail? Why? Why? Why?" No, instead, I can say, "It's not your fault you're an obese pig. It's your bone structure. You've got big bones, a big frame. You'll never be skinny or petite. Don't blame yourself. Go have a milk shake and cheer yourself up." Who am I kidding? Nobody but me. But it helps. I saw this old movie once on TV, "Lost Weekend," about this alcoholic. His moment of truth comes when he's sitting in a bar and he sees that it's his hand that's lifting the drink to his mouth, that he's the one controlling both his hand and his mouth. I know the same things, but I'm not always ready to stop eating. Maybe I haven't taken a good enough look at myself. Maybe in a dressing room I'll take a true, good look someday and then I'll know, like the alcoholic knew, I have only myself to blame. Thanks, Mom, for trying to be a scapegoat and for giving me bone structures and genes to blame, but I know it's me. Honest.

.   .   .   .

This student's first freewriting enabled her to develop an idea for her second freewriting, which turned out to be a very powerful and self-revealing piece of writing. Had she continued on, she might have found another topic for a third freewriting in her second freewriting, and so on. The beauty of freewriting is that it is easy to do and each freewriting opens up a wealth of ideas for further writings.

Freewriting #1

Freewrite for ten or fifteen minutes on why you feel so many myths and misperceptions surround writing and the writing process. Write freely, following the natural flow of your ideas. Do not stop the flow of your writing to correct, edit, or revise your work.

_____

_____

_____

_____

_____

_____

_____

_____

_____

_____

_____

_____

_____

_____

_____

_____

_____

_____

Group Exercise #1

To test the hypothesis that written language is crucial for clear and accurate communication, try the following exercise.

One person in each group will be selected by the teacher as the message giver (MG), whose responsibility it will be to bring to class a message of moderate complexity, such as one might find in a business memo, a sales brochure, or a newspaper or magazine article. The message should average 100-150 words and should include specific information about names, dates, special events, and so on.

The message giver (MG) is encouraged to bring his or her own message for this exercise. One appropriate message might be as follows:

- Opponents of the Morgan City Rapid Transit System have rejected Morgan City's plan for a $1 billion, 93 mile rail and downtown subway system designed to connect the suburbs with the downtown Central Business District (CBD). The group, led by former Morgan City mayor Milton "Bud" Gravely, said that the City Council needs to look carefully at its demographics for the suburbs, urging them to be aware that population growth in the suburbs has exceeded estimates for the past ten years by nearly 27%. The City Council's figures indicate a much slower rate of growth than what Gravely anticipates will be the case in the next fifteen years. Thus, the rapid transit system might be outdated before its construction is even completed, and new revenue measures will have to be undertaken to bring the system in line with population needs and trends. Gravely urged acceptance of the Miller-Holzbein proposal, in which funding for the rapid transit system would be extended over a twenty-year period and financed, in part, from revenues from the new tollway that connects Morgan City with Cassaday County.

The MG brings the message to class but does not share it with anyone until the activity begins. At this point, the class (or group members) should separate from the MG, either by going outside the classroom and waiting in the hall, or by going to the back of the classroom so that conversation will not be overheard.

The MG then calls one person forward and instructs that person to read the message and take a few moments to absorb its details. That person will then tell what he or she can remember of the message to the next person in line.

The key idea here is that the first person will try to convey the message to the second person from memory only and will not share the written message with the second person. Likewise, the second person will tell the third person in line what he or she remembers, and so on, until all the members in the class or the group have had the message passed on to them. When the message has completed its journey of repetitions and recountings, the last person to hear the message will write down what he or she has heard and then tell the rest of the class what message he or she received. Comparisons will then be made (in the groups or in the class) between the original and the final messages.

Invariably, the messages will differ in some surprising ways. Not only will little details have been lost, but often the sense of the passage will be altered in bizarre or absurd ways. The obvious message is that writing enables us to communicate with an accuracy and precision that is simply impossible in oral exchanges.

In the space that remains, describe how the message you heard changed from its initial version to the final. Then speculate on how those changes might have affected the situation or context from which the message was taken.

_____

_____

_____

_____

_____

_____

_____

_____

Exercise #2

Choose <u>one</u> of the following statements and, in the space below, answer the questions asked.

Do you agree with the statement, "Every time you use your writing ritual will make the next time you write just that much easier"? What might there be about rituals that might make it easier for you to write the next time, and the next?

OR

Describe what, for you, would represent the ideal writing ritual. Are there ways in which your ideal writing ritual conflicts with your present writing ritual? If so, why do you think that might be? What solutions do you propose for resolving that conflict?

_____

_____

_____

_____

_____

_____

_____

_____

_____

_____

_____

_____

_____

_____

Freewriting #2

Write for a few minutes, explaining your views and feelings about freewriting. So far, is it a valuable tool for opening up your creative thinking? Why might that be? In what ways might you be able to use freewriting in your own writing habits to stimulate creativity and thinking? In what ways might it not work?

_____

_____

_____

_____

_____

_____

_____

_____

_____

_____

_____

_____

_____

_____

_____

_____

_____

_____

_____

Point/Counterpoint: Considering Alternative Arguments

The purpose of this section is to introduce you to an important concept in critical thinking--the refutation. The idea of the refutation is that truth often is rarely simple or clear-cut and that arguments, statements, and premises can and should be seen from a number of angles or points of view.

To think critically, you must question and challenge statements that are presented as facts to you. A good place to begin your critical reading and thinking is by cross-examining statements that appear in your textbooks. In each of the exercises that follow, you are asked to respond to one of the ideas presented to you in your writing textbook or in this critical thinking journal. <u>Your task is to assess the merit of these ideas</u> by probing the strengths and weaknesses of the statements. If the case made for the original argument, position A, seems interesting and convincing, how will considering the opposite viewpoint, position B, affect your view of A?

These Point/Counterpoint exercises will help you look at ideas from a number of perspectives and thus teach you to critically examine claims for their truth, accuracy, and relevance.   Choose <u>one</u> of the following exercises and write your responses in the space provided.

1. On the opening page of Chapter One, a student describes what for him seems to be a fairly successful "writing ritual"--gathering up all his materials, getting on his bike, riding to campus, and setting himself up in the art lounge in the student center.   No distractions.   Quiet.   The camaraderie of other people hard at work.   A different setting and different surroundings.

What do you think of this "writing ritual"? Do you think the ritual itself--the leaving home and going to the student center in the evenings--has as much to do with the writing itself, or is it the dedicated commitment to getting his work done that makes this student's ritual so successful? Do you agree with the idea that to get your writing done you would have to give your writing some measure of time and focused attention? Does that mean moving to a special, designated place? Why might that be?

2. In Chapter One, Stephen Reid, the author of your textbook, gives you one model of how the writing process works and of how writers go about

that process: writing rituals, keeping journals, lots of warm-up exercises like freewriting to get you started.

Do you agree with this model? Is this the way you go about your writing? Does this model seem, to you, more appropriate to people who are "stuck" and don't know how to begin, than to people with a strong sense of conviction about what they want to write? Suppose someone really angered you and you had to write back a response. Would you go through the process Reid describes in writing your response? Would you need a writing ritual? Would you need a lot of freewriting exercises? Similarly, suppose you were excited and wanted to tell somebody how thrilled you were about receiving first prize in a contest. Would Reid's model of the writing process still apply?

3. In describing his model of the writing process, Reid uses quotations from a number of writers, including Gore Vidal, Doris Lessing, Ernest Hemingway, Edna O'Brien, Gabriel Garcia Marquez, Gloria Steinem, Margaret Atwood, Maria Irene Fornes, Ntzoake Shange, Donald Murray, Toni Cade Bambara, and E. M. Forster, to support his position. Most of these authors, ten out of twelve, are creative writers--novelists, short story writers, or playwrights; the remaining two, Gloria Steinem and Donald Murray, are essayists.

Keeping a journal seems to be of value to creative writers, but do you think keeping a journal is more appropriate to creative writers, who often depend on memory and accurate descriptions of a range of details for their writing, than it is to other types of writers?

Do you feel that keeping a journal would work for other types of writing, or other types of settings? Like business or technical writing, for example? Would you find much value in keeping a journal if you were working and writing in a business or professional setting? If you wouldn't find a journal of much help in this setting, could you imagine any type of writing exercises or practices that you would find of value?

Summary and Assessment Page

What ideas from Chapter One: Myths and Rituals (in either your textbook or your critical thinking journal) helped you the most with your writing? What ideas or techniques did you hope to get from this chapter but did not? What steps do you intend to take to learn those ideas or techniques?

_____

_____

_____

_____

_____

_____

_____

_____

_____

_____

_____

_____

_____

_____

_____

_____

_____

_____

_____

Chapter Two: Purposes and Processes for Writing

Many students think of writing as a procedure, with a straightforward, unvarying set of steps to follow, rather than as a process. Viewing writing as a procedure, they want simple guidelines or blueprints they can follow with little deviation from a set plan.

If writing were a procedure, like let's say changing a flat tire or putting together a model airplane, it would be easy to specify the steps one would follow. First you do this, then you do that; follow steps one, two, three, four, five, six, seven, eight, nine, and then, *voila*, the well-made essay! Wouldn't that be grand?

Indeed, it would, but writing is not a procedure. In fact, the belief that writing is a procedure is one of the most limiting and pervasive myths about writing. The view that writing is a procedure, however, can be a very comforting one, and one that many students find attractive. The belief that writing can be procedurized makes writing seem simpler, somehow, and manageable. Learn the procedure and write like a professional. Sounds almost like a magazine ad, doesn't it? "For $19.95, you, too, can get the <u>Writing Procedure Manual</u> and write like a pro! Hurry now and place your order. If you call before 5:00 p.m., we'll throw in a set of steak knives and a bamboo steamer absolutely free!"

Sounds too good to be true, doesn't it? And that's because it is. Only in a very few instances does writing follow a procedural form, and often these are examples of business and technical writing (such as memos, certain types of business letters and reports, and instructional manuals) in which the focus is on simple, instructional writing. This type of writing lends itself rather easily to a formulaic organizational pattern. Most other types of writing, though, do not.

The alternative to viewing writing as a procedure is to view it as a process. A process suggests an ongoing movement, while a procedure suggests a predetermined set of steps to follow or a procedure that is static and relatively unchanging. Procedures, too, are largely impersonal. They are structured in such a way that anybody who follows this set of steps or directions will come out with the same anticipated result. In contrast, a process often not only invites but almost necessitates a high degree of personal investment. The creative energy and uniqueness of the individual are what make a process flow.

So when you begin your writing process, don't depend too much on procedures or set plans to carry you through. Your writing process will allow you to be creative, as long as you are flexible enough to follow a new idea. So as you write, look for that moment of discovery or surprise, when your writing takes a different turn than the one you expected. That's when your writing process may really pay off.

Exercise #1

In this chapter, your textbook says that "most good writing has a personal dimension. It may be about the writer's personality or it may address a subject or an idea the writer cares about. It begins in honesty, curiosity, inquiry, and vulnerability. . . . By continually probing and learning, being honest with themselves, and accepting the risks, writers can use their writing to teach themselves and others."

The idea of a "personal dimension" is related to the concept of a writer's voice. Turn to Chapter Four, Remembering. Read the two paragraphs in that chapter about "Voice and Tone."

Now, close the book and explain below what you think "personal dimension" and "voice" mean. How are they related? How are they different?

_____

_____

_____

_____

_____

_____

_____

_____

_____

_____

_____

_____

_____

_____

_____

Exercise #2

Return to your textbook and reread one of the following three essays: "Writing for Myself," "The Struggle to Be an All-American Girl," or "I'm OK, but You're Not."

In the essay you've reread, how would you define the writer's voice? Does this essay possess a "personal dimension" to its style and structure? How would you explain the relationship between the writer and the intended audience?

_____

_____

_____

_____

_____

_____

_____

_____

_____

_____

_____

_____

_____

_____

_____

_____

_____

_____

_____

Freewriting #1

Find one essay you have written in the last two years. Using one of your essays for specific examples, discuss your writing in terms of your own "personal voice." Find two or three sentences that you think reveal your voice. Does writing in a "personal voice" come easily to you? Have you been encouraged by others, especially your teachers, to write in a "personal voice," or have you been encouraged to be more formal and objective in your writing?

Group Exercise #1

Here is a good way for the class to check out the hypothesis that a logical plan of organization is essential to the quality of an essay's achievement. In this exercise, the class is divided into groups of four or five, and each group is asked to evaluate the merit of four essays written in response to the topic of whether the writer agrees with or disagrees with French philosopher Jean-Paul Sartre's statement, "We are our choices."

Each of the essays should be evaluated for the merit of quality of its structure, as well as for the quality and depth of its argument. Does the essay exhibit a logical plan of organization, and, secondly, is the essay's argument convincing?

Each group should evaluate the essay using any method it chooses, although awarding grades (A-F) is the common practice. After the essays have been evaluated, each group will write a paragraph explaining how they evaluated and assessed each essay's structure and, based on their analysis, what constitutes good structure in an essay.

Essay #1 "Choices"

I agree with Sartre's statement. I mean, what else could we be but our choices? We choose the kind of food we eat, and I heard on the news the other day that certain kinds of diets can cause diseases like cancer and heart trouble. This would be an example of how our choices could affect who we are. I know from experience that the food you eat can have an effect upon you. I am allergic to wheat, and whenever I eat wheat I break out in a rash. If I made a different choice, I wouldn't get sick.

It's not just food that is part of the choices we make. There are also jobs. If I study to be an engineer, that's a choice I make. There are also marriage and children. You choose these things, and that's why I think Sartre is right about our choices making us who we are.

Money is another area where there's a lot of choice. My uncle Harry lost a lot of money investing in stocks. He bought stock in a meat processing company, and it went bankrupt. Nobody made him do that, and he'd be the first one to say it was his own fault.

So, from the idea that we control the food we eat, the way we dress, the jobs we have, and whether we have marriages and children, I would agree with Sartre's statement that we are our choices.

Essay #2 "Is it Really Up to Us?"

If you could be anything you wanted to--what would you be? Would you be the same, or would you drastically change? Jean-Paul Sartre states, "We are our choices." If this were true, wouldn't we all be millionaires, fashion models, or something more exciting than the position we presently occupy? I have to disagree with Sartre. I feel that there are certain limitations to what we can do and therefore become.

While Sartre would say that a person's life is shaped by the choices he or she makes, I believe a person's life is just as influenced by things over which he has no control. For example, the main limitations that hinder a person in pursuit of his choices are circumstances (or fate, if you will) and an individual's abilities. These two barriers are often extremely hard, if not impossible, to change. Therefore, I feel we tend to make compromises about our choices and settle for the best possible situation. For instance, Joe wants to go to college and land a fantastic job upon graduation. However, Joe's family is financially troubled and unable to put him through college. On the other hand, suppose Joe receives financial aid enabling him to attend. Joe receives failing marks in all classes because his academic skills are weak. In the first situation, Joe's environment is limiting his choices, just as his academic ability, or lack thereof, would have rendered Joe unable to graduate. It turns out that Joe is good with engines and he decides to work in that field. He is able to make some money for the family and is relatively happy. I believe many people fall prey to this type of "compromise and settle" pattern. I wish to pilot airplanes but can't because of my poor eyesight. A handicapped child wants to run, skip rope, or dance, but is unable. Each individual is unique. It is this uniqueness that is the separating factor in the choices that each individual has to make.

I agree with Sartre's basic ideas on the impact of choice. However, I feel that Sartre would argue that the compromise or reevaluation of a choice is a choice in itself. I disagree; rather, I would argue that our lives are made up of a series of compromises stemming from our limited choices. Sartre may also argue that I have misinterpreted his original meaning of choice. He may be speaking of the choices that each individual makes after he discovers his limitations. I extracted from Sartre's quotation, "We are our choices," a rather holistic ideal that we can choose and therefore become anything we desire. Instead of the idea that we are our choices, aren't our choices or types of choices dictated by the limitations upon us?

Essay #3 "Sartre's Philosophy"

Sartre is right. Many of the choices we make do influence our lives. I am a living example of that. I chose to leave home at sixteen and support myself instead of letting my parents support me. I wanted to be independent and provide for myself. I got a job working as a switchboard operator at a hospital, and I moved in with my sister until I finished high school. By then I had enough money to have my own apartment. I got a scholarship to college because I had good grades in high school. Now I am majoring in nursing and hoping to be a registered nurse someday. If I could not make my own choices, I would not have been able to go out on my own, go to college, and become a nurse someday.

I think Sartre is right, we are our choices.

Essay #4 "Stick to Philosophy"

Jean-Paul Sartre is a philosopher, and only a philosopher could make a statement like "we are our choices" because philosophers deal in abstractions and life is not an abstraction.

I ate a pizza for dinner tonight. Did I choose to eat that pizza of my own free will, or was I influenced by the "Let Yourself Go" ad that Pizza Hut had on TV? A $30 million dollar a year advertising budget is enough to get anyone in there munching down pizza--are these people making choices or responding to Pavlovian conditioning?

If I can't even eat pizza of my own free will, how am I going to make the even bigger choices in life--like who am I going to be, what am I going to believe, what kind of lifestyle do I want, and how will I find personal fulfillment in life? Aren't I going to be batted around like some shuttlecock here, too? Aren't I going to decide it's neat to wear Polo shirts because of Ralph Lauren's multi-million dollar ad campaigns, and aren't I going to be influenced about being a sensitive male-like Alan Alda or Bill Cosby--or a macho brute, like Don Johnson or Sylvester Stallone, depending upon what image of the male my society approves of at any given moment? I'm probably going to be a pretty typical guy. I'm going to shave every morning or wear a beard (whatever's in vogue), put on the best-selling cologne, work, grab up my copy of GQ to read on the bus, train, or subway to work, and the whole time think I am freely making choices and also free to make those choices.

C'mon, Mr. Sartre. Come into the real world. We're products of a media age--our lives are shaped, molded, defined, and packaged by commercial interests who have their pocketbooks and not our best interests in mind. We are our choices? Baloney. We're carbon copies of what the ad campaigns tell us to be. Even if we revolt, we do so in the most predictable ways--the punk rockers look alike, the druggies rot out their brains in search of elusive dreams, the motorcycle gangs have their own sense of "vogue" and what's "in" or "out." It's the same stuff, either way you cut it. Join in and wear your Guccis, or drop out and dye your Mohawk hairdo pink, purple, or green. Are these choices? No, these are people being manipulated into believing they have choices to make.

C'mon, Jean-Paul. I'll take you to Pizza Hut. We'll order a Deluxe pan pizza with everything on it and extra thick crust. We'll drink Classic Coke and watch big-screen MTV. Then we'll discuss this foolish idea you have about how we are our choices.

Exercise #3

Review some of the papers that you have written for previous classes, either in high school or in college. Take a look at your introductory paragraphs and at the logical plan of development each paper offers. Based on your analysis, critique your work and write a profile of yourself as a writer, focusing on strengths and weaknesses. How do you feel you have changed as a writer from these earlier papers until now? What areas have you improved in but still need additional work?

_____

_____

_____

_____

_____

_____

_____

_____

_____

_____

_____

_____

_____

_____

_____

_____

_____

_____

Point/Counterpoint: Considering Alternative Arguments

Respond to <u>one</u> of the following sets of questions.

1. Reread the opening paragraphs of this chapter in your critical thinking journal. What does it mean to you to say that writing is a process and not a procedure? How do you define these two terms in relationship to writing? How would your view of writing change if you viewed it as a procedure? A process? Do you think this distinction is an important one? What does this distinction mean to you and your view of writing?

2. Do you feel that your textbook presents you with a view of writing as a procedure or a process? What evidence within the textbook leads you to this conclusion? Explain.

3. With a friend you discuss what you have been learning in your composition class, and she says to you, "I think the distinction being drawn between procedure and process is a meaningless one. A process is only a procedure with more variations and options." Write out your response to this statement.

_____

_____

_____

_____

_____

_____

_____

_____

_____

_____

_____

_____

Summary and Assessment Page

What ideas from Chapter Two: Purposes and Processes for Writing (in either your textbook or your critical thinking journal) helped you the most with your writing? What ideas or techniques did you hope to get from this chapter but did not? What steps do you intend to take to learn those ideas or techniques?

_____

_____

_____

_____

_____

_____

_____

_____

_____

_____

_____

_____

_____

_____

_____

_____

_____

_____

_____

Chapter Three: Observing

Observation, or the act of recognizing and noting a fact or occurrence, is intrinsically related to the creative processes involved in writing. So, too, are the judgments or inferences to be drawn from what one has observed, and it is here that a great deal of the insight associated with observation resides.

Psychologist Rollo May considers the inferences to be drawn from observation as a type of intimate seeing that is unique and personal to each individual observer. He also describes this process as an involvement with and a penetration into reality that is invariably the <u>starting point of creativity</u>. As May states in "Creativity and Encounter":

> Creativity occurs in an act of encounter, and is to be understood with this encounter at its center. Cezanne [an impressionist painter] sees a tree. He sees it in a way no one else has ever seen it. He experiences, as he no doubt would say, a "being grasped" by the tree. The painting that issues out of this encounter between a person, Cezanne, and an objective reality, the tree, is literally new. Something is born, comes into being, something which did not exist before--which is as good a definition of creativity as we can get. Thereafter everyone who has the experience of encounter with the painting, who looks at it with intensity of awareness and lets it speak to him, will see the tree with the unique powerful movement and the architectural beauty which literally did not exist in our relation with trees until Cezanne experienced and painted them.

What May is describing is a type of experiential consciousness, or a consciousness that is keenly aware of its experiences and the possibilities they contain. Awareness of events, occurrences, and details, together with the ability to draw insightful inferences from this data, are what May identifies with the creative process.

Exercise #1

How would you relate May's concept of seeing and observing to the one presented to you by your textbook? Are they similar or dissimilar? Do they complement each other or contradict one another? Which of the two views of observing (May's or your textbook's) do you prefer and why?

_____

_____

_____

_____

_____

_____

_____

_____

_____

_____

_____

_____

_____

_____

_____

_____

_____

_____

_____

Exercise #2

Your textbook makes a distinction between objective and subjective seeing or observation. <u>Choose an object or place and describe it both objectively and subjectively</u>. What differences do you notice in these two approaches? How do these two approaches affect your writing, especially the "voice" or personal dimension of your writing?

_____

_____

_____

_____

_____

_____

_____

_____

_____

_____

_____

_____

_____

_____

_____

_____

_____

_____

_____

Group Exercise #1

The teacher or a student selected for this exercise brings to class a cardboard box full of objects. The objects may come from the person's home or any other location, and they may be chosen at random or by design. The objects themselves are to be varied, but they may range from the most common and everyday, like a leaf, to the most unique or exotic.

On the day of the exercise, the person removes the objects from the box and places them on a desk or table for the class to see. The class will then write a short descriptive essay about the items from the box using their powers of observation and combined with their interesting musings or reflections upon the objects in order to produce an engaging, speculative essay.

_____

_____

_____

_____

_____

_____

_____

_____

_____

_____

_____

_____

_____

_____

Exercise #3

Below is another selection from Dinesen's <u>Out of Africa</u>. Consider this selection in terms of its powers of description and its selective use of details. On the next page, answer the following questions: Is this a well-written and effective description? What makes it so? What aspects of description, such as sensory details, comparisons and images, and focus on a dominant idea, does Dinesen use in this passage? How do these techniques work together in this passage to create the passage's mood and its effects upon the reader?

There are times of great beauty on a coffee-farm. When the plantation flowered in the beginning of the rains, it was a radiant sight, like a cloud of chalk, in the mist and the drizzling rain, over six hundred acres of land. The coffee-blossom has a delicate slightly bitter scent, like the blackthorn blossom. When the field reddened with the ripe berries, all the women and the children, whom they call the Totos, were called out to pick the coffee off the trees, together with the men; then the waggons and carts brought it down to the factory near the river. Our machinery was never quite what it should have been, but we had planned and built the factory ourselves and thought highly of it. Once the whole factory burned down and had to be built up again. The big coffee-dryer turned and turned, rumbling the coffee in its iron belly with a sound like pebbles that are washed about on the sea-shore. Sometimes the coffee would be dry, and ready to take out of the dryer, in the middle of the night. That was a picturesque moment, with many hurricane lamps in the huge dark room of the factory, that was hung everywhere with cobwebs and coffee-husks, and with eager glowing dark faces, in the light of the lamps, round the dryer; the factory, you felt, hung in the great African night like a bright jewel in an Ethiope's ear. Later on the coffee was hulled, graded and sorted by hand, and packed in sacks sewn up with a saddler's needle.

Then in the end in the early morning, while it was still dark, and I was lying in bed, I heard the waggons, loaded high up with coffee-sacks, twelve to a ton, with sixteen oxen to each waggon, starting on their way in to Nairobi railway station up the long factory hill, with much shouting and rattling, the drivers running beside the waggons. I was pleased to think that this was the only hill up, on their way, for the farm was a thousand feet higher than the town of Nairobi. In the evening I walked out to meet the procession that came back, the tired oxen hanging their heads in front of the empty waggons, with a tired little Toto leading them, and the weary drivers trailing their whips in the dust of the road. How we had done what we could do. The coffee would be on the sea in a day or two, and we could only hope for good luck in the big auction-sales in London.

_____

_____

_____

_____

_____

_____

_____

_____

_____

_____

_____

_____

_____

_____

_____

_____

_____

_____

_____

_____

_____

Freewriting #1

Right now, wherever you are as you read this page, stop for a moment and look around you. Write down, on this page, the details of whatever you notice, whatever descriptive ideas, words, phrases come to your mind. Jot down your ideas as quickly as they come, and strive for a complete a list of descriptive terms as you can create. When you run out of ideas, study your surroundings again, as though you were trying to paint each detail. Then continue writing.

_____

_____

_____

_____

_____

_____

_____

_____

_____

_____

_____

_____

_____

_____

_____

_____

_____

_____

_____

_____

Freewriting #2

Try the same exercise as in Freewriting #1, but this time, let the focus of your writing be upon something from your memory, not an object or place immediately present to your eyes. Again, your focus should be on describing a single scene, object, setting, or person. (Do not narrate an event.)

_____

_____

_____

_____

_____

_____

_____

_____

_____

_____

_____

_____

_____

_____

_____

_____

_____

_____

_____

_____

Exercise #4

Compare what you wrote in Freewriting Exercises #1 and #2. Which came more easily to you, the one that focused on your immediate surroundings, or the one you wrote from memory? Why do you think that might be?

Did you notice any difference in the way you <u>felt</u> as you were jotting down your ideas for these two writings? Did you find yourself more personally invested in the writing you did from memory than in the writing that described your immediate surroundings? Why do you think that might be? Do you think these two writing exercises might touch on the issues raised by the differences between objective and subjective descriptions? Why might that be?

_____

_____

_____

_____

_____

_____

_____

_____

_____

_____

_____

_____

_____

_____

Exercise #5

Excellent descriptive writings generally combine a keen eye for detail with an ability to draw interesting and insightful inferences from the details observed. For this exercise, you will combine observed detail with inferences.

Specifically, you are to (1) observe and record the details of a place or setting identified with the tastes or preferences of an individual and (2) draw inferences about what the person might be like, based upon the details you have observed. A good example might be a student's dorm room, which is decorated with posters, pictures, and memorabilia that say a great deal about what the student likes, values, and feels identified with.

_____

_____

_____

_____

_____

_____

_____

_____

_____

_____

_____

_____

_____

_____

_____

_____

Point/Counterpoint: Considering Alternative Arguments

Write your response to two of the following questions.

1. Suppose an individual you met were to insist that the distinction made between objective and subjective description is an artificial one, since no act of description by an individual can ever exclude that individual's particular way of looking at, interpreting, and understanding the world; therefore, all description is, at its heart, subjective, even though it might appear to take on an objective surface or cast. How would you respond to this individual?

2. Do you consider the following selection from W. Somerset Maugham's *Rain* to be an example of subjective or objective description? Why?

> She was a little woman, with brown, dull hair very elaborately arranged, and she had prominent blue eyes behind invisible pince-nez. Her face was long, like a sheep's; but she gave no impression of foolishness, rather of extreme alertness; she had the quick movements of a bird. The most remarkable thing about her was her voice, high, metallic, and without inflection; it fell on the ear with a hard monotony, irritating to the nerves like the pitiless clamor of the pneumatic drill.

3. Your textbook states that "observing is essential to good writing." Do you agree? Do you think that this is true of all types of writing, or only descriptive writing?

4. Your textbook emphasizes that "describing what is <u>not</u> there" is an important aspect of observation and description.   "Keen observation requires, sometimes, stepping back and noticing what is absent, what is not happening, who is not present." Do you agree? How would you apply this concept to the passages in the text from Dinesen and Dillard?

5.   Return to the <u>Observing Objects</u> section of your textbook and reconsider the description by Paul Goldberger of the two types of cookies, the sugar wafer and the fig newton. Goldberger elaborates a very complex analysis from these cookies that focuses upon their socio-political implications as man-made objects in the modern world. What do you think of Goldberger's analysis? Do you think it is perceptive or contrived? Do you think Goldberger has presented an interesting point of view that leads to greater insights, or do you feel he has overstated his case--that, for example, there are times when a cookie is only a cookie?

6. Your textbook states that spatial order and chronological order can be effective methods for organizing essays. Others might disagree, suggesting that these methods are too formulaic and predictable and therefore lead to dull, lackluster writing. Do you agree or disagree with this second view of organizing essays by spatial and/or chronological order?

_____

_____

_____

_____

_____

_____

_____

_____

_____

_____

_____

_____

_____

_____

_____

_____

_____

_____

_____

_____

Summary and Assessment Page

What ideas from Chapter Three: Observing (in either your textbook or your critical thinking journal) helped you the most with your writing? What ideas or techniques did you hope to get from this chapter but did not? What steps do you intend to take to learn those ideas or techniques?

_____

_____

_____

_____

_____

_____

_____

_____

_____

_____

_____

_____

_____

_____

_____

_____

_____

_____

_____

_____

_____

Chapter Four: Remembering

Here is a way to conceptualize the lasting and interesting effect memory has upon our lives. Think of a song that you have heard in two distinct time periods and phases of your life. Perhaps there was a love song that was very popular at the time you were graduating from high school that you heard again recently on the radio. Has your sense of that song changed now that you are older and no longer in love? Can you conceptualize two sets of memories surrounding that song, one set that involves happiness and fond memories because you were in love, and one set that brings back sad memories because of the loss of that love? Isn't it interesting that one song can bring back both a happy and a poignant feeling as you hear it, and both of those feelings are representative of important moments and phases in your life?

This is the essence of memory. Not only does it enable us to recall very vivid and meaningful events in our lives, but it also allows us a double perspective upon those events. The Christmas song you associate with your family as a child will have a different meaning to you as you grow older and see your family in a new light. In the same manner, the song will take on even greater meaning when you have a family of your own and play that song for your children. Memory enables us to keep track of our lives and to be aware of the changes we have gone through in becoming who we are.

As you write about your memories, then, look for a double perspective, a memory point/counterpoint. Try to find some point of difference or change in your beliefs or attitudes that might focus your memory. The tension or sense of surprise created by what you once thought or felt at one point in time versus what you now think or feel may lead to the main point or idea for your essay.

Freewriting #1

Freewrite about the ways that you might use memories to enhance your writing. What do you think it is about memories that adds a special and unique touch to writing, especially to descriptive writings and narration?

_____

_____

_____

_____

_____

_____

_____

_____

_____

_____

_____

_____

_____

_____

_____

_____

_____

_____

_____

_____

Group Exercise #1

Each person should bring to class pictures of himself or herself at different points in life: perhaps a childhood photograph, a photograph from elementary or high school days, and a recent photograph. Each person will then write out a short essay based upon what he or she was like in each of these photographs. How did the person in each of these photographs view life? What were the important issues surrounding his or her life at the time? What were some happy moments for this person, and some disappointments? How has his or her perspective on life changed from the earliest photograph to the most recent?

The class members should then hold up the photographs of themselves and share the memories associated with each phase. Class members should answer the question, "If I knew then what I know now, I would have. . . ." If the passages written about the photographs are not too intensely personal, let each person read out loud what he or she has written and share these reflections with the class.

Exercise #1

Memory is more than a handy device to help you recall names and places, faces and dates. Memory is a highly valued intellectual skill, especially in our contemporary era of information processing in which there are vast amounts of material associated with almost any profession one might choose.

Contemporary theorists tend to divide memory into three components: skill, verbal response, and emotional response. Skill involves our ability to recall what we have learned to do, like ride a bicycle, for example. We may learn this skill in June and apply it again in July. We are able to do this because we can remember the skill that we have learned. If we were unable to do this, we would have to relearn everything each time we wanted to do something! A monumental and time-consuming task, at best.

Verbal response is what most of us generally think of when we consider memory, for verbal response involves the ability to recall a specific event or idea, like who was the first president of the United States, what date and time our next appointment is with the dentist, what recipe to follow in making lasagna, etc. This aspect of memory, like the ability to recall a skill, is one that can be improved through concentration, practice, and the use of certain techniques to aid recall.

Emotional response, however, as the name suggests, involves our feelings about certain events or experiences. A person, for example, might learn to be afraid of snakes, and that fear can stay with the person for all of his or her life--far beyond the duration of the first immediate encounter with the snake itself.

Another way of rephrasing what contemporary theorists say about memory is to say that we learn to do (skill), to say (verbal response), and to feel (emotional response). Obviously, this gives a very large and important role to memory in our lives, since it affects every aspect of our consciousness.

Explain your response to these contemporary theories. Do you agree that emotional responses stay with a person longer than verbal responses? Why might that be? Does the learning required in college courses rely only on verbal response, or does it require doing and feeling as well? Why might that be? In this course, which of these types of memory do you draw upon as you write?

_____

_____

_____

_____

_____

_____

_____

_____

_____

_____

_____

_____

_____

_____

_____

_____

_____

_____

_____

_____

Exercise #2

In the <u>Prologue</u> to *The Way to Rainy Mountain*, N. Scott Momaday writes:

The journey herein recalled continues to be made anew each time the miracle comes to mind, for that is peculiarly the right and responsibility of the imagination. It is a whole journey, intricate with motion and meaning; and it is made with the whole memory, that experience of the mind which is legendary as well as historical, personal as well as cultural. And the journey is an evocation of three things in particular: a landscape that is incomparable, a time that is gone forever, and the human spirit, which endures. The imaginative experience and the historical express equally the traditions of man's reality. Finally, then, the journey recalled is among other things the revelation of one way in which these traditions are conceived, developed, and interfused in the human mind.

In this passage, Momaday makes a clear connection between memory and the imagination. Do you think that memory and imagination are integrally related? Why? Can the imagination function without memory? Can memory function without imagination? Explain your own definition of the imagination.

_____

_____

_____

_____

_____

_____

_____

_____

_____

_____

_____

Exercise #3

In the previous passage, Momaday expresses a deep respect for the land (landscape) and its influence upon memory and imagination. Further in his book, he also states: "I came to know that country, not in the way a traveler knows the landmarks he sees in the distance, but more truly and intimately, in every season, from a thousand points of view. . . . Once in his life a man ought to concentrate his mind upon the remembered earth, I believe. He ought to give himself up to a particular landscape in his experience, to look at it from as many angles as he can, to wonder about it, to dwell upon it."

Is there a particular place (or landscape) that you feel a strong attachment to, the kind of empathy and respect that Momaday describes for his landscape? Why do you feel you might have such a strong attachment to that place? Is the actual place different from the landscape of the place you have created in your mind? Why do you think that might be?

How would you describe this place to another person in such a way that he or she could sense and feel the emotional pull this place had upon your life and memory? Do you think some people are more affected by a sense of place than others are? Why do you think that might be?

_____

_____

_____

_____

_____

_____

_____

_____

_____

_____

_____

Freewriting #2

Now try writing about your sense of a landscape, a place, as a freewriting. As you write, think about the following questions: Is there a shift in your focus or feelings as you freewrite about this topic? Does the use of freewriting here enable your "voice" to be more personal and self-disclosing than in a piece of writing directed toward an audience?

_____

_____

_____

_____

_____

_____

_____

_____

_____

_____

_____

_____

_____

_____

_____

_____

_____

_____

_____

_____

Exercise #4

Read the following selection from Maya Angelou's autobiography, *I Know Why the Caged Bird Sings*. Author and poet, Angelou grew up in Stamps, Arkansas, and was raised by her grandmother (who is referred to in the selection as Sister Henderson). With her brother Bailey and her Uncle Willie, Angelou lived in the back of her grandmother's country store, which she describes as her "favorite place to be."

. . . .

Weighing the half-pounds of flour, excluding the scoop, and depositing them dust-free into the thin paper sacks held a simple kind of adventure for me. I developed an eye for measuring how full a silver-looking ladle of flour, mash, meal, sugar or corn had to be to push the scale indicator over to eight ounces or one pound. When I was absolutely accurate our appreciative customers used to admire: "Sister Henderson sure got some smart grandchildrens." If I was off in the Store's favor, the eagle-eyed women would say, "put some more in that sack, child. Don't you try to make your profit offa me."

Then I would quietly but persistently punish myself. For every bad judgment, the fine was no silver-wrapped Kisses, the sweet chocolate drops that I loved more than anything the world, except Bailey. And maybe canned pineapples. My obsession with pineapples nearly drove me mad. I dreamt of the days when I would be grown and able to buy a whole carton for myself alone.

Although my syrupy golden rings sat in their exotic cans on our shelves year round, we only tasted them during Christmas. Momma used the juice to make almost-black fruit cakes. Then she lined heavy soot-encrusted iron skillets with the pineapple rings for rich upside-down cakes. Bailey and I received one slice each, and I carried mine around for hours, shredding off the fruit until nothing was left except the perfume on my fingers. I'd like to think that my desire for pineapples was so sacred that I wouldn't allow myself to steal a can (which was possible) and eat it alone out in the garden, but I'm certain that I must have weighted the possibility of the scent exposing me and didn't have the nerve to attempt it.

Until I was thirteen and left Arkansas for good, the Store was my favorite place to be. Alone and empty in the mornings, it looked like an unopened present from a stranger. Opening the front doors was pulling the ribbon off the unexpected gift. The light would come in softly (we faced north), easing itself over the shelves of mackerel, salmon, tobacco, thread. It fell flat on the big vat of lard and by noontime during the summer the grease had softened to a thick soup. Whenever I walked into the Store in the afternoon, I sensed that it was tired. I alone could hear the slow pulse of its job half done. But just before bedtime, after numerous people had walked in and out, had argued over their bills, or joked about their neighbors, or just dropped in "to give Sister Henderson a 'Hi y'all,'" the promise of magic mornings returned to the Store and spread itself over the family in washed life waves.

.   .   .   .

In the space below, freewrite about the following questions: What do you think Angelou's purpose might be in writing this description? What perspective do you feel Angelou adopts in narrating this piece, that of the child, or of the adult? Which of the senses does Angelou use in her description? What comparisons and images can you find? What values and attitudes does Angelou describe for herself, her grandmother (Sister Henderson), and for the townspeople? How do these attitudes and values contribute to the effect of the piece? What main idea or feeling does Angelou convey to you about the store and her life in Stamps, Arkansas?

_____

_____

_____

_____

_____

_____

_____

_____

_____

_____

_____

Point/Counterpoint: Considering Alternative Arguments

Write out your response to two of the following issues.

1. Do you feel that writing from memory is important? Why? How would you respond to a person who views writing from memory only as self-indulgent and overly emotional?

2. Your textbook states that voice "refers to a writer's personality as revealed through language" and suggests that the "personal voice," which is very much about human feelings and emotions, is often the most appropriate one for writing from memory. Ben and Tom have just left a composition class that discussed the idea of "voice" in writing. Ben says to Tom, "I don't see the value of all this emphasis upon a 'personal voice' in writing. That's all well and good for people who are going to be creative writers, but what about people like me? I'm going to be an engineer, and I'll never need to use a 'personal voice' in my career. I feel like I'm wasting my time. What I need to learn is the type of impersonal tone or voice that will give my professional writing an air of scientific objectivity."

How would you respond to Ben's objections?

3. The essay on trash day by Kurt Weekly presented in your textbook illustrates one view of the value of writing about remembered events. Often this process can have a cathartic effect, relieving people of pent-up emotions and frustrations and freeing them from the pain of unresolved emotional conflicts. Often clients in therapy are encouraged to write from their memories, keeping a journal of the events that have shaped their personalities and a record of their changing perspectives about their life experiences.

Do you agree with this perspective of the value of writing about remembered events? Have you ever found it of value in your own life? Do you believe that writing about a remembered event might give a person an opportunity to connect with the deepest of "inner voices" and write honestly about a troublesome experience? Do you feel that memories are the "inner voice" within a person? Why do you think that might be?

4. Your textbook emphasizes dialogue as one aspect of writing about remembered events.   Maya Angelou incorporates a small amount of

51

dialogue into her description of life in the Store. How do you feel her essay would have changed if more dialogue had been included? Do you think it would have made the essay stronger or weaker to include more dialogue? Why?

_____

_____

_____

_____

_____

_____

_____

_____

_____

_____

_____

_____

_____

_____

_____

_____

_____

_____

_____

_____

Summary and Assessment Page

What ideas from Chapter Four: Remembering (in either your textbook or your critical thinking journal) helped you the most with your writing? What ideas or techniques did you hope to get from this chapter but did not? What steps do you intend to take to learn those ideas or techniques?

_____

_____

_____

_____

_____

_____

_____

_____

_____

_____

_____

_____

_____

_____

_____

_____

_____

_____

_____

_____

Chapter Five: Reading

Freewriting #1

How do you see the connections between writing and reading? In what ways do you usually think about or accommodate your reader as you write a paper? Write about an experience you have had reading something that you found difficult to follow. How did that writer help or fail to help you as a reader?

_____

_____

_____

_____

_____

_____

_____

_____

_____

_____

_____

_____

_____

_____

_____

_____

_____

Reading

Sometimes it might seem that reading is a very isolated, private task--that it occurs almost in a vacuum. You usually do it alone, when it is quiet, because it is difficult to focus on what you are reading when other people are talking or listening to music around you. Their distractions and noise make it difficult to concentrate. They definitely are not helping you read.

But in many important ways, reading is really a social activity. While reading academic materials, you are engaged in a "conversation" with the author of the piece--and quite probably with other authors who have written on similar topics. You are bringing your own prior experiences to the text and trying to construct meaning from the writer's words. The writer is also engaged in a conversation with other writers who have already written about the same subject. You are included in this ongoing conversation, and you are being asked to form your own opinions about the subject of this conversation. Thus, you are <u>collaborating</u> with the writer of your text, with the goal of creating a meaningful exchange of ideas.

Now let's look at the writer's side of this reading/writing conversation. As a reader, you work with the writer to make meaning, but as a writer, you must work with your reader to get the conversation going. Since writers and readers must collaborate to create meaning, you must consider your reader as you write. The problem is that--unlike an actual, live conversation--you cannot stop and ask your reader, "Do you understand this point?" "What questions do you have so far?" Since you cannot talk to your reader directly, you must learn to <u>anticipate</u> the kinds of questions and reactions that readers might have. For example, what experiences are your readers likely to bring to the text you are creating? What meanings or reactions will your audience form as they read your words? Where do you need to give lots of examples to illustrate your point? As the textbook suggests, good writers give signals to their readers, so that readers can make better guesses about what is coming. Good writers also use examples from their personal experience in the hope of activating their readers' prior knowledge. Good writers help their readers make the connections that make conversations possible.

Exercise #1

As your book explains, reading depends upon the reader's prior experiences and prediction to create comprehension. Read <u>only the opening two paragraphs</u> of the following three essays: Barbara Ehrenreich's "Teach Diversity--with a Smile," David Quammen's "Animal Rights and Beyond," and Deborah Tannen's "How Male and Female Students Use Language Differently" (see Chapter Seven for text of essay).

Then write down your predictions: What will be the main <u>subject</u> of the essay? What is the author's <u>thesis</u> or argument? How will the author <u>organize</u> or develop the essay? What will the author use for <u>evidence</u> or support?

After you complete Group Exercise #1, check to see how accurate your predictions were.

_____

_____

_____

_____

_____

_____

_____

_____

_____

_____

_____

_____

_____

_____

_____

_____

Exercise #2

Being able to accurately summarize what you have read in written sources is an extremely important reading skill. In previous chapters and writing exercises, you used both observation and recollection as the basis for your writings. Now the focus shifts, and you will move into a type of writing that is more characteristic of most of your academic courses and certainly of the business and professional world.

This change to a different source of materials for your writing should not be uncomfortable for you. You will not be abandoning skills you have learned; you are only adding to your repertoire of abilities. The two predominant skills to learn will be the ability to restate a written passage in your own words (paraphrasing) and the ability to abstract the main ideas from a passage (summarizing). This exercise will explain how to write summaries and paraphrases, and it will then ask you to write a summary of Neil Petrie's essay in Chapter Two of your text.

Students often confuse these two key skills, thinking that a paraphrase is a summary, or that a summary is a paraphrase. In a similar fashion, students often think that a summary includes every example, every fact, and every statistic when, actually, a summary reduces the size of the original material and focuses on the main ideas, not the examples or data.

The purpose of a paraphrase is to convert a difficult and complex passage to a more simple statement of the writer's main ideas. A paraphrase usually simplifies and clarifies a passage from an original article or essay. Typically, you may summarize the main ideas of a whole article, but paraphrase (put in your own words) a short passage or two from the original. Often, writers use some paraphrase as they write a summary, abstract, or precis of the original material.

A summary begins with a statement of the author and title of the material being presented. Then it states the main ideas. In order to present the main ideas, however, you have to have a clear idea of the meaning of the whole passage. One way to do this is to underline key words and phrases as you reread the material. After you've underlined key words, write all the main ideas in the margins of the passage. Finally, note any key phrases that you might want to quote directly--but don't quote long sentences. (As you take notes, remember that a summary does not include specific facts, examples, or data in the original.) With the key words, the main ideas, and a few important quotations, you're ready to write your summary.

Before you begin to write, however, decide on the length of your summary. If you're given an assignment such as "Summarize the following passage in one hundred words or fewer," then your summary must be brief and precise. If you do not have an assigned length, however, you may want to aim for 200-300 words or one-fourth of the length of the original --whichever is more appropriate.

As you actually draft your summary, occasionally refer to the author's name using identifying phrases that remind your reader that you are citing the author's ideas, not your own. In a summary of the Petrie essay, for example, you should include tag phrases such as "According to Petrie," "as Petrie argues," "Petrie suggests that," or "as the author says."

For this exercise, reread the essay by Neil Petrie in Chapter Two of your text. Underline key words, write out the main ideas in the margin as you reread, and note phrases that you may wish to quote directly. Then, beginning with a sentence that cites the author and the title, summarize Petrie's essay in 200-300 words. Use the space remaining on this page for your notes.

_____

_____

_____

_____

_____

_____

_____

_____

_____

_____

_____

_____

Group Exercise #1

Divide into groups of three or four and compare your predictions about the three essays from the previous exercise. First, choose one of the three essays.

Individually, read and annotate the chosen essay, noting the main points. Then, as a group, draft an objective summary. Be sure your summary does the following:

- Cite the author and title of the essay.

- Indicate the main ideas of the essay.

- Use direct quotation of key words, phrases, or sentences.

- Include author tags, such as "According to Tannen . . ."

- Do not use specifics or data unless they are central to the essay's main point.

- Remember to represent the author's ideas accurately and fairly. Save your responses and opinions for your response.

After each group has finished the summary, compare summaries from different groups to see how differently the ideas come through. Note that although much of the summary will be the same, different readers or groups of readers may present slightly different views of each essay.

Now check the accuracy of your own predictions from Exercise #1. Where were your predictions most accurate? Where were your guesses off the mark? Cite one passage where the author needed to give better clues. Cite one of your predictions where you misread or simply guessed wrong. How could the opening paragraphs be changed to help readers anticipate more accurately?

Exercise #3

Reread your chosen essay, this time annotating it based on your responses to the author's ideas. You may note areas where you <u>agree or disagree</u>; where you feel the argument is particularly <u>strong or weak</u>; or where you <u>interpret or reflect on</u> the author's ideas. Imagine that your essay is a conversation between you and the author--what responses would you make during that conversation? Try to come up with at least one comment from each of the above types of responses.

After annotating the text, arrange your points into a double column log. Use Paula Fisher's double entry log at the end of the chapter as a model. Then draft your response to the essay, making sure to include a transition to indicate that you are no longer summarizing.

Description	Response

Agree/Disagree:

Analysis of text:

Interpret/Reflect:

Group Exercise #2

Read and annotate the Deborah Tannen essay, "How Male and Female Students Use Language Differently" (see Chapter Seven for text of essay). As a group, consider Koester's and Browe's responses to the Tannen article. After discussing the article in your group, synthesize Koester's and Browe's responses and draft a revised response which shows both the strong and weak points of Tannen's essay.

Your group may revise, modify, or change any of Koester's or Browe's arguments as you draft your synthesized response to Deborah Tannen's essay. Use the space below to outline the strengths and weaknesses that your revised essay will discuss.

_____

_____

_____

_____

_____

_____

_____

_____

_____

_____

_____

_____

_____

_____

_____

Point/Counterpoint: Considering Alternative Arguments

1.   In the opening quotation for the chapter, David Bartholomae and Anthony Petrosky, authors of *Ways of Reading*, have this to say:

> Reading involves a fair measure of push and shove. You make your mark on a book and it makes its mark on you. Reading is not simply a matter of hanging back and waiting for a piece, or its author, to tell you what the writing has to say.

Explain what this statement means. How, for example, can you "shove" or "push" something that you read? How do you "make your mark" on a text? Explain why you agree or disagree with the above quotation.

2.   Your author, Stephen Reid, says that there are three dimensions to reading: <u>reading</u>, <u>writing</u>, and <u>discussing</u>.   But can't you read something and understand it without writing about it?   And can't you read something and understand it without discussing the ideas with others?   Pick out a novel or a textbook you are currently reading.   Use your reading of that text to explain why you agree or disagree that reading has three dimensions.

3.   This chapter explains that the reading process is based on the following theory:

Prior Experience	+	**Predictions**	=	**Comprehension**
About the subject About language About culture		Guesses about how the text relates to prior experience; Predictions about the text's direction		Making meaning; Understanding the text

Explain why you agree or disagree with this theory.   For example, do you always make predictions when you read?   Can't you just read something and understand it? And if two of the important dimensions of reading are writing and discussing the text with others, why don't writing and discussing fit in this equation somewhere?

4.   Why does reading have to have a theory, anyway?

Summary and Assessment Page

What ideas from Chapter Five: Reading (in either your textbook or your critical thinking journal) helped you the most with your writing? What ideas or techniques did you hope to get from this chapter but did not? What steps do you intend to take to learn those ideas or techniques?

_____

_____

_____

_____

_____

_____

_____

_____

_____

_____

_____

_____

_____

_____

_____

_____

_____

_____

_____

_____

_____

Chapter Six: Investigating

Freewriting #1

In the previous chapters, your critical thinking journal has begun with a summary of key ideas from the text, along with some additional ideas to consider. Now, you should begin practicing this exercise yourself. After you have read the opening pages of the text, close the book. Without consulting the text, write out the major ideas you remember.

_____

_____

_____

_____

_____

_____

_____

_____

_____

_____

_____

_____

_____

_____

_____

_____

_____

_____

_____

_____

_____

Freewriting #2

After you complete Freewriting Exercise #1, reopen your textbook. Review the opening pages of the chapter for not more than five minutes. Close the book again. Now compare what you wrote in your first freewriting to what you discovered in rereading the opening pages of the text. Below, write out any new ideas, corrections, or additions to your first notes. What did you misunderstand on your first reading? What did you forget to include?

_____

_____

_____

_____

_____

_____

_____

_____

_____

_____

_____

_____

_____

_____

_____

_____

_____

_____

_____

Investigating

Your textbook suggests that investigation begins with questions to uncover truths not generally known or accepted. In the process of investigating, you (1) discover facts and information from key sources; (2) select and organize that information for your audience; and (3) report that information in a lively and easily understood manner. Remember that a report does <u>not</u> argue for or against any idea, issue, or theory.

Essays reporting information share certain features in common. For one, obviously, they have a <u>thesis</u> they wish to present to an audience, as well as an interesting <u>angle</u> or slant toward their subjects. Like all essays, the thesis in an informative essay must be narrowed so that the topic is not so broad that an audience is overwhelmed with information and cannot follow what is being discussed.

Second, a good informative essay <u>appeals to your audience's interests</u>. You must determine how much your audience is likely to know already about your topic so that the information you give them is relevant and new. If you bore your audience by repeating information they already know, you may lose your audience. If, on the other hand, you exclude key bits of information, you run the risk of confusing your audience. If you are writing about cellular biology to a general, lay audience who has little knowledge of biology, you cannot write your piece with a wealth of terminology, facts, and statistics that only biology specialists would understand. What about cellular biology might interest my readers? What might they be curious about? What about cellular biology will influence my audience's lives? What might be the value or application of the information I have to share with them?

Third, informative essays must clearly <u>explain any technical or specific terms vocabulary</u>. For example, if you are writing about the mining industry and black lung disease and you use the term <u>alveoli</u>, you must clarify for a general audience that you are discussing air sacs in the lungs. Without this definition, there is the potential that the whole point of your discussion will be lost to your audience.

The fourth point to remember is that good informative essays have an underlying logical <u>plan of organization</u>. Facts and details thrown at a reader in a relatively random fashion will not be interesting or memorable. Facts marshaled together to support a central point will be. Often investigative essays provide a wealth of information and a large number of facts and details. To be effective, investigative essays must divide the information into parts or categories that make sense and support the main thesis. Divisions suggest, too, that transitions between the various parts must be clear and give a clear sense of flow to the ideas.

Often when one has worked on an investigative piece for a long time, the information seems very clear simply because of the amount of exposure the writer has had to the material. Never forget, though, that your reader will be trying to grasp your information for the first time. Often what seems so crystal clear to you will not be very clear to your reader unless you organize well and give lots of transitions and signals. Anticipate possible rough spots and leave nothing to chance. That way you will avoid a whole range of possible misunderstandings or misinterpretations that might obscure your message and negate all your hard work.

Freewriting #3

Freewrite for ten or fifteen minutes about your own processes of investigating and finding out facts. Write about a specific time in your life when you investigated and researched information in order to make an informed decision. Perhaps you were writing an essay, perhaps you were shopping for an important purchase, or perhaps you were looking for a job or choosing a college. How did your investigative processes help clarify your decision-making processes?

_____

_____

_____

_____

_____

_____

_____

_____

_____

_____

_____

_____

_____

_____

_____

_____

_____

_____

_____

_____

Group Exercise #1

This exercise is an investigation of transitions and how they work in writing. Like all investigations, it involves gathering and interpreting data.

Each person will bring to class one short selection from writings he or she admires. The class will divide into groups of three or four people and read and discuss each selection. Groups should pay particular attention to introductions, main ideas, and transitions. The essay that exhibits the best transitions, in each group's opinion, will be presented and discussed as a model for the class to study and learn from as they write their own essays.

Group Exercise #2

Investigating begins with finding accurate facts and information, but it also requires drawing <u>valid conclusions</u> or <u>inferences</u> from the facts you do find. The facts do not speak for themselves. Writers must draw conclusions that follow logically from the given facts or statistics.

In this exercise, your group should determine what conclusions can logically be drawn from the following data. What conclusions does your group reach? Which of these conclusions seem most logical and sound? What additional data would your group need to draw meaningful conclusions? Be prepared to explain your choices to the rest of the class.

1. During the 1960s and 1970s, the divorce rate in America nearly doubled. The 1960s and 1970s were also the era in which the greatest gains were made for the Civil Rights movement and for the Women's Liberation movement.

2. Cityview has one of the highest crime rates in America. When a survey is conducted, it is discovered that the Cityview municipal water supply is one of the three most polluted water supply systems in America. It is also discovered that Cityview residents buy 14.5% more toy machine guns, space weapon systems, and laser beam rockets as gifts for their children than residents of other cities in America with equivalent populations.

3. Fifty-seven robberies of convenience stores occur in Townesville, U.S.A. The police investigate, locate, and arrest the criminals involved. As the police compile their data for their crime reports, they discover that 36% of those arrested for the convenience store robberies were high on marijuana at the time, 11% were high school dropouts, and 63% were wearing red shirts at the time of the robbery.

Group Exercise #3

Your class should arrange itself into groups of three persons. Two people in the group should then interview the third person. Their goal is to gather information so they can write a brief profile of that person. Their profile should contain some basic biographical information but it should <u>focus</u> on one special skill or area of expertise that that person has. The audience for this profile will be other members of the class. After the first two people have finished taking notes, group members should change roles and interview the other two members of the group. When the interviews are completed, group members should be prepared to present a profile of one of their group members to the rest of the class.

Group Exercise #4

The purpose of this exercise is to investigate slang words used by your group members and report your findings to the class.

As you interview each other, collect examples from several categories of slang. For example, one category might be contemporary slang understood by all members of a peer group. In this category might be words such as "dude," "wired," "lame," or "awesome." A second category of slang words might be words given special meanings by individuals. One group came up with the following "personalized" vocabulary: "oleagenous" (a bad move in sports, i.e., a move that looks like oleo); "heinous" or "the hein" (really excellent); and "crumbing" (do poorly or fail). Finally, you might investigate vocabulary related to a particular activity or sport. One group investigated frisbee language and came up with the following: "gitis" (a cross-body, under-the-leg catch); "crash and burn" (aerial catch and fall); "scud" (a throw that goes a long way but is not very accurate); and "brain motel" (a series of frisbee moves so complex that the brain "checks in but doesn't check out").

At the end of 15 minutes, be prepared to report your findings to the class. Remember that you should be collecting examples of slang, but you should also be looking for some information about slang that other class members don't already know or for information that might surprise them.

Point/Counterpoint: Considering Alternative Arguments

Choose two of the following issues and write your responses.

1. What is your sense of the value of investigative writing? How do you differentiate investigative writing from other kinds of writing, like description, narration, process analysis, etc., that are also designed to convey information to a reader?

2.   "Investigative writing begins with questions to uncover truths not generally known or accepted." Do you agree? Why or why not?

3.   Professor Southworth, in discussing investigative writing with her composition class, states, "The ideal of investigative writing is that all investigations be thorough and as unbiased as humanly possible. The reality, unfortunately, is very much different in that most investigative pieces are not very thorough and only give as much background material as is necessary to get the piece going and, as for bias on the part of the investigator, that's a built-in assumption in all investigative pieces. The truth is, class, that the investigator slants the approach and the findings in the direction that he or she chooses and reports the results that support these views while minimizing or overlooking results that would support the opposing views." Do you agree with Professor Southworth's views? Why or why not? Did you read any essays or passages from essays in Chapter Five that support or refute Professor Southworth's view?

4. Of the techniques of investigative writing presented to you by your textbook and your critical thinking journal, which one would seem (or has proven) to be the most helpful to you? Which one the least helpful? Why might this be, in both instances?

5.   Are there future instances or situations in which you can foresee writing investigative pieces? What might those situations be? If you cannot perceive yourself ever doing any this of investigative writing, do you feel your study of the methods and requirements of investigative writing has been a waste of your time? Why or why not?

_____

_____

_____

Summary and Assessment Page

What ideas from Chapter Six: Investigating (in either your textbook or your critical thinking journal) helped you the most with your writing? What ideas or techniques did you hope to get from this chapter but did not? What steps do you intend to take to learn those ideas or techniques?

_____

_____

_____

_____

_____

_____

_____

_____

_____

_____

_____

_____

_____

_____

_____

_____

_____

_____

_____

_____

Chapter Seven: Explaining

Freewriting #1

As you did at the beginning of Chapter Six, read the opening pages of Chapter Seven: Explaining and then close your text. Below, write out the main ideas you remember from those pages.

_____

_____

_____

_____

_____

_____

_____

_____

_____

_____

_____

_____

_____

_____

_____

_____

_____

_____

_____

Freewriting #2

Now, go back and reread the opening pages of Chapter Seven. Then, read the next page in your critical thinking journal about Explaining.

Below, jot down any main ideas from these two passages you did not summarize on the previous page. In addition, write out any <u>questions</u> about explaining that occurred to you while you were rereading the passages or doing your freewriting.

_____

_____

_____

_____

_____

_____

_____

_____

_____

_____

_____

_____

_____

_____

_____

_____

_____

_____

Explaining

At this point in the course, you need to stop for a moment and reflect on the kinds of writing that you have already done and the kinds you will do later. The first four main chapters (Observing, Remembering, Reading and Investigating) helped you practice drawing on the major <u>sources</u> of information and ideas. Those sources are listed below:

Observing: Drawing on observed sensory detail about the world.

Remembering: Drawing on your recollections and memories.

Reading: Reading actively, summarizing, and responding.

Investigating: Drawing on written sources, interviews, and
                observations.

At this point in the course, you will start combining all four of these sources, as necessary, as you write for specific purposes. Now you need to think how your observations, your memories, and the information you gather from books and from interviews can have a particular <u>effect</u> on your audience. You need, in other words, to think about the <u>purpose</u> of your writing. The major purposes are listed and described below:

Informing: Selecting and organizing facts and data for an
           audience.

Explaining: Interpreting information in order to show what
           something is, how it happens or should happen,
           and/or why something happens.

Evaluating: Persuading your reader to accept your judgment
           about the value or worth of something.

Problem Solving: Persuading your reader to accept your
           analysis of a problem and your recommendation
           to solve the problem.

Arguing: Persuading your reader to accept your claim about
           what something is, why something happens, what
           something is worth, or how to solve a problem. In
           arguing, you persuade by supporting your claim and
           <u>refuting</u> any alternative or opposingclaims.

Group Exercise #1

The class should divide into groups of four or five and use the following paragraphs and questions to discuss informing, explaining, and arguing as purposes for writing. Each person in the group should read the following paragraphs and answer questions 1-3 for himself or herself. Then, the group should discuss their responses and reach consensus responses for each question. A group recorder should take notes on the group's discussion and their consensus answers. Finally, the group should be prepared to report their findings to the rest of the class.

The distinctions among the various purposes for writing may not seem particularly obvious or clear. Take, for example, the differences between informing as a purpose and explaining as a purpose. Are they really about the same? Or are there distinct differences? Then consider the difference between explaining and arguing. How exactly are they different? Read the following explanation and then comment on whether you (1) understand the definitions, (2) agree or disagree that informing, explaining, and arguing are distinct and separate purposes, and (3) agree or disagree that knowing about the distinctions among these purposes will help you as a writer.

The Investigating chapter in your textbook states that as a result of your investigation, you will report your findings to a specific audience. Reporting your findings means that you will inform your audience about what you have learned. The words "reporting" and "informing" suggest that the writer is presenting to a specific audience certain facts, data, and ideas that the writer has found in the process of investigating. The idea of reporting evokes the journalistic standard of recording and transmitting what the reporter finds in a fair and relatively objective manner. In a newspaper article, for example, the reporter should not comment on, editorialize, argue for or against, or otherwise interpret the main ideas, facts, and events. Of course, pure objectivity is a fiction, since no person can report events without some element of subjectivity, bias, or point of view. Even a television camera is not completely objective, since the camera operator interprets by selecting the subject and determining the field of vision. Although no writing is completely objective, reports or writing intended to inform readers do strive to eliminate bias and interpretation by relying accurately on key sources: written articles and documents, interviews, surveys, and first-hand observation. By being faithful to sources, by citing sources accurately, and by endeavoring to assume a non-editorial or non-argumentative tone and stance, writers can fulfill the purpose of providing readers with information that they may need.

Explaining as a purpose for writing involves an intentionally higher degree of interpretation than does informing. In order to explain what something is, how it happens, or why it happens, writers of explaining essays begin with the information they find on the subject, but they are now free to offer their own understanding of the ideas or process. They acquire all the information that the reporter uses, but now they must give their own (not someone else's or some source's) explanation or interpretation of what something means, how it works or should work, and why it happens. To write an explaining essay, then, writers find relationships among the bits of information. They synthesize the information. They (rather than their sources) do the thinking, and they present their findings as their own ideas, rather than merely quote the ideas of some expert.

To illustrate the difference between informing and explaining, consider the following example. A local newspaper might contain a report on the homeless in a community. The report gives information gathered from statistics, from welfare agencies, and from city government sources. The writer of a report focuses primarily on these sources rather than his own or her own ideas. In contrast, in an explaining essay on the homeless, the writer is free to use all the information gathered from newspaper reports as he or she explains and interprets the statistics, comments on the validity of interview comments, and contrasts statistical information with first-hand observation. The writer of the essay explains (i.e., interprets) the relationships among the bits of information.

Finally, in an arguing essay, a writer concentrates on advocating a particular claim or interpretation as the best interpretation or most effective proposition. Writers of arguing essays use information as they do their research and they must explain key relationships among the facts they find, but their ultimate purpose is to persuade an audience to believe in their claim or to act on their claim. In the process of persuading readers, writers of arguing essays must anticipate and respond to alternative or opposing arguments.

Informing, explaining, and arguing thus form a sequence of purposes that gradually become more complex and gradually involve more interpretation and commitment on the part of the writer. Informing, explaining, and arguing are a like a series of Chinese boxes with arguing being the largest box, explaining the next smaller, and informing the smallest. Arguing "contains" instances of explaining and informing; similarly, explaining "contains" bits of informing. The reverse, however, is not necessarily true. A writer can inform without offering his or her own explicit interpretation, explanation, or argument. Similarly, a writer can explain an idea or a process without attempting to refute other competing or conflicting explanations.

Exercise #1

Explaining essays have a thesis or main idea. This thesis is the main point for the whole essay. Usually, writers do not know what this main point is until they have done some collecting, shaping, or even writing. As they read and write, writers of explaining essays keep looking for one clear main idea that brings everything into focus. This statement may answer the reader's question, "So what?" or "Why are you telling me this?" Often this "So what" idea is the thing the writer learns or discovers during the writing process. The key here is the sense of discovery--the element of surprise. What the writer learns or is surprised by often becomes the thesis.

Choose one of the professional or student samples in Chapter Seven: Explaining. Find the thesis or main idea of that essay. Does this sentence contain a discovery--for you or possibly for the writer? Does it contain a surprise? Is there a sense of "Ah-ha!" embedded in the thesis sentence? Explain.

_____

_____

_____

_____

_____

_____

_____

_____

_____

_____

_____

_____

Exercise #2

As you read expository writing, you should learn to understand and identify the "rhetorical situation" of the passage. The rhetorical situation includes knowing who the author is, why the passage was written, who the intended audience is, what the subject of the passage is, and what the main point or thesis is.

You won't be able to learn all of this information without some historical or background information, but you can make some guesses based on each of these excerpts. For example, even if you don't know that Francis Bacon was a 16th century English philosopher and essayist, you can gather from the diction (word choice) that his selection was written several hundred years ago. You can also guess from his voice that he is a scholar who engages wittily yet seriously with his subject.

Read the following four passages. Then, citing specific phrases from each passage to support your answer, respond to the following questions:

(1) Who is the author and/or what does the voice of the passage reveal about the author?
(2) What is the purpose of the passage? What might have prompted the author to write each passage?
(3) Who is the intended audience? Who might be most interested in the author's explanation?
(4) What is the subject and what is the main idea or thesis of the passage?

a) David Feldman, Who Put the Butter in Butterfly?

Why Does Buck mean "a Dollar"?

Buck has meant "male deer" since the year 1000 in England and has meant "a dollar" in America since 1856. Despite the time gap, the two meanings are closely linked. In the early eighteenth century, traders and hunters used buckskin as a basic unit of trade. Any frontiersman who possessed many buckskins was considered a wealthy man.

How did buck come to mean specifically one dollar? In the early West, poker was the diversion of choice. A marker or counter was placed to the left of the dealer to indicate who was the next to deal. This marker was traditionally called the buck, because the first markers were buckhorn

83

knives. But in the Old West, silver dollars (i.e., one dollar), instead of knives, were used as bucks.

The buck as poker counter yields the expression pass the buck, a favorite of politicians and bureaucrats everywhere, who usually are more than happy to evade responsibility for governing, dealing poker, or just about anything else, which was why it was so surprising to hear Harry Truman, an admitted poker player, announce, "The buck stops here."

b) Natalie Goldberg, *Writing Down the Bones: Freeing the Writer Within*

Writers live twice. They go along with their regular life, are as fast as anyone in the grocery store, crossing the street, getting dressed for work in the morning. But there's another part of them that they have been training. The one that lives everything a second time. That sits down and sees their life again and goes over it. Looks at the texture and details.

In a rainstorm, everyone quickly runs down the street with umbrellas, raincoats, newspapers over their heads. Writers go back outside in the rain with a notebook in front of them and a pen in hand. They look at the puddles, watch them fill, watch the rain splash in them. You can say a writer practices being dumb. Only a dummy would stand out in the rain and watch a puddle. If you're so smart, you get in out of the rain so you won't catch cold, and you have health insurance, in case you get sick. If you're dumb, you are more interested in the puddle than in your security and insurance or in getting to work on time.

c) Howard Ensign Evans, "The Story of Fireflies"

The light organs of fireflies are complex structures, and recent studies using the electron microscope show them to be even more complex than one supposed. Each is composed of three layers: an outer "window," simply a transparent portion of the body wall; the light organ proper, and an inner layer of opaque cells filled with granules of uric acid, the so-called "reflector." The light organ proper contains large, slablike light cells, each of them filled with large granules and much smaller nerves penetrating the light organ. These smaller granules were once assumed by some persons to be luminous bacteria, but we now know they are mitochondria, the granules that fill most of the light cells are still of unknown function; perhaps they serve as the source of luciferin.

d) Francis Bacon, "Of Studies"

Studies serve for delight, for ornament, and for ability. Their chief use for delight is in privateness, and retiring; for ornament, is in discourse; and for ability is in the judgment and disposition of business; for expert men can execute, and perhaps judge of the particulars, one by one; but the general counsels, and the plots and marshaling of affairs, come best from those that are learned.

To spend too much time in studies, is sloth; to use them too much for ornament, is affectation; to make judgment wholly by their rules, is the humor of a scholar; they perfect nature and are perfected by experience-- for natural abilities are like natural plants, that need pruning by study; and studies themselves do give forth directions too much at large, except they be bounded in by experience. Crafty men condemn studies, simple men admire them, and wise men use them, for they teach not their own use; but that is a wisdom without them, and above them, won by observation.

Read not to contradict and confute, nor to believe and take for granted, nor to find talk and discourse, but to weigh and consider. Some books are to be tasted, others to be swallowed, and some few to be chewed and digested; that is, some books are to be read only in parts; others to be read, but not curiously; and some few to be read wholly, and with diligence and attention. Some books also may be read by deputy, and extracts made of them by others; but that would be only in the less important arguments, and the meaner sort of books; else distilled books are like common distilled waters, flashy things.

Reading maketh a full man, conference a ready man, and writing an exact man; and, therefore, if a man write little, he had need have a great memory; if he confer little, he had need to have a present wit; and if he read little, he had need have much cunning, to seem to know that he doth not. Histories make men wise; poets, witty; the mathematics, subtle; natural philosophy, deep; moral philosophy, grave; logic and rhetoric, able to contend.

Freewriting #3

In your dictionary, look up the meaning of "education." Write down the dictionary's definition. Then freewrite on the idea of education, answering the following questions: What does education mean to you? How have you or how should one go about getting an education? Why should one get an education? (Or, What are the effects of having a good education?)

_____

_____

_____

_____

_____

_____

_____

_____

_____

_____

_____

_____

_____

_____

_____

_____

_____

_____

_____

_____

Freewriting #4

In your text, reread the section on <u>analogy</u> in your text (see Chapter Four: Remembering). Then reread the passage you wrote in your last entry about education. Think of an analogy you could use to explain what an education is, how to get a good education, or why one should get an education. Write out your analogy below.

_____

_____

_____

_____

_____

_____

_____

_____

_____

_____

_____

_____

_____

_____

_____

_____

_____

_____

_____

_____

Point/Counterpoint: Considering Alternative Arguments

Read the following questions and write your response to two of them.

1. Which of the techniques for writing explanatory essays presented to you by your textbook and your journal seemed to you the <u>most</u> helpful? Which were the <u>least</u> helpful? Why do you think that might be?

2. Your critical thinking journal made distinctions between writing to <u>inform</u>, writing to <u>explain</u>, and writing to <u>persuade</u> or argue. Reread the explanation. Isn't the difference between writing to inform and writing to explain really splitting hairs? Aren't they really the same? And what about explaining versus arguing?   When you are trying to explain something, aren't you really trying to persuade your reader that your interpretation is correct?   What is the purpose or reason for these distinctions, anyway?

3. In an explanatory comment of your own, explain the value of the techniques of branching, observing, remembering, investigating, shaping, defining, classifying, comparing, contrasting, drawing analogies, and analyzing processes to the writing of explanatory essays. If you had to eliminate any two techniques from the list above, which <u>two</u> would you eliminate as the least important? Why?

4. Return to your textbook and reread the selection by psychologist Sukie Colgrave from <u>Spirit of the Valley: Androgyny and Chinese Thought</u>. Colgrave states that "the experience of being 'in love' is one of powerful dependency."

Do you agree?   Why or why not?   How would you explain dependency in this context? What do you think Colgrave means by the term? If you had to explain this term through an analogy, what analogy would you choose? Explain the reasons for your choice.

5. Explain which part of the discussions on explaining presented in either your textbook or your critical thinking journal do you think were not explained very well, or at least not as clearly as other sections? In what ways were they unclear? How could they be made more clear? Explain.

Summary and Assessment Page

What ideas from Chapter Seven: Explaining (in either your textbook or your critical thinking journal) helped you the most with your writing? What ideas or techniques did you hope to get from this chapter but did not? What steps do you intend to take to learn those ideas or techniques?

_____

_____

_____

_____

_____

_____

_____

_____

_____

_____

_____

_____

_____

_____

_____

_____

_____

_____

_____

_____

_____

_____

Chapter Eight: Evaluating

Exercise #1

After reading the opening pages of Chapter Eight: Evaluating, make notes
to yourself that you could use to explain to your class the meaning of the
following terms: <u>evaluating</u>, <u>criteria</u>, <u>overall claim</u>, <u>standard of judgment</u>,
and <u>data</u> or <u>evidence</u>.

_____

_____

_____

_____

_____

_____

_____

_____

_____

_____

_____

_____

_____

_____

_____

_____

_____

_____

_____

Evaluating

"A claim or opinion," your textbook states, "is not an evaluation." One of the primary ways that an evaluation differs from an opinion is that an evaluation is based on carefully gathered <u>evidence</u>. Your opinion is something that you express and your reader or listener either accepts or rejects. Your evaluation, on the other hand, should provide enough evidence so that the reader is persuaded that your claim is fair and valid.

Evaluation depends on evidence, and evidence often consists of both <u>examples</u> and <u>statistics</u>. Both examples and statistics can be derived from your own experience and from research that you do for an assignment. Examples are individual instances, set in a specific time and place, that support larger generalizations. To evaluate fairly, you must use your examples fairly. If you see one work-study student who is not doing a good job on your campus, it is neither fair nor accurate to argue that all work-study students are lazy and incompetent. This viewpoint seems highly self-evident, but you'd be surprised how many people jump to hasty conclusions based on one incident or example.

An example gives a specific instance, while statistics are numerical summaries of specific instances or pieces of information. Statistics can be very convincing in an evaluation. If you find, for example, that 87% of all Yugo owners were dissatisfied with their "frequency or repair rate" for their cars, this can be a much more convincing and valid piece of data than telling the example of Joe Jones who had his Yugo in the shop 91 days out of 365 days last year. While Joe's case is the part of the statistics you are quoting, the impact of the larger numbers attached to the statistics may be more powerful and convincing than the narrating of the one case that Joe represents.

On the other hand, statistics can often be dry and unappealing, while an example often has the personal touch that your reader can relate to. Human beings don't experience life statistically; they live, and make judgments, one experience at a time. A specific example that itemizes the long list of troubles that your friend Joe encounters, beginning with the alternator, the handbrake, and the starter motor and ending with the automatic transmission, the brake linings, the clutch, and the engine valves begins to add weight and authenticity to your evaluation. In addition, if your example narrates <u>one specific time</u> when Joe's Yugo broke down in heavy traffic, and other motorists were shouting at him, and he was out in a heavy downpour, leaning under the hood trying to fix the carburetor--

then the reader gets a vivid and memorable picture of the problems he or she might encounter with a Yugo.

When appropriate, writers of evaluations use both statistics and examples. The statistics give their evaluation a sense of reliability and validity and the specific examples show readers how human beings actually reacted to the subject being evaluated.

Exercise #2

Reflect for a moment on the ways that you make judgments and formulate opinions and beliefs. If possible, think of one recent instance when you made a judgment about some person, thing, or event. What do you think were the strongest factors that influenced your belief? Do you consider yourself an open-minded individual, one who is receptive to new ideas, or do you feel you are pretty set in your opinions and beliefs? Why do you think that might be? Do you feel most people are fairly open-minded or closed-minded in their beliefs? Why do you think so?

_____

_____

_____

_____

_____

_____

_____

_____

_____

_____

_____

_____

_____

_____

_____

_____

_____

Exercise #3

The class or group should bring in examples of advertisements that rely on slogans, pictorial representations, and/or data that are favorable to the product and perhaps misleading to the consumer. Let each group discuss the ways in which each advertisement does or does not do a fair job of evaluating its product or service. How would each ad need to be revised or rewritten to make the evaluation accurate, fair, or valid? Each group should discuss one advertisement and be prepared to present their findings to the rest of the class.

_____

_____

_____

_____

_____

_____

_____

_____

_____

_____

_____

_____

_____

_____

_____

_____

_____

Exercise #4

Write out a sentence containing a possible standard of judgment (or criterion) for each of the following statements:

Sample: The college I attend is an excellent school.

One possible standard of judgment or criterion: An excellent school is one that places a high value on the classroom education of its undergraduate students.

1. Paradise Cafe is the best restaurant in town.

2. This novel is the worst book I've ever read.

3. Professor Brown is an excellent economics teacher.

4. Ronald Reagan will be judged by history to be one of our best presidents.

5. Gun control is a good idea for our society to pursue.

6. Money can't buy happiness.

Note: Is your standard of judgment debatable? If so, how might someone else write a standard of judgment that would support the opposite judgment?

_____

_____

_____

_____

_____

_____

_____

Exercise #5

Read the following excerpt from "Pragmatism," an essay by William James, and evaluate the merit or truth of what James is saying. Do you agree or disagree with his perspective?

Truth lives . . . for the most part on a credit system. Our thoughts and beliefs "pass," so long as nothing challenges them, just as banknotes pass so long as nobody refuses them. But this all points to direct face-to-face verifications somewhere, without which the fabric of truth collapses like a financial system with no cash basis whatever. You accept my verification of one thing, I yours of another. We trade on each other's truth. But beliefs verified concretely by <u>somebody</u> are the posts of the whole superstructure.

James says that "beliefs verified concretely by <u>somebody</u> are the posts of the whole superstructure [of Truth]." Based upon your study of evaluation, what methods, in your opinion, would seem to work best at verifying beliefs or judgments? What are some methods you might suggest that could be used to verify facts or beliefs?

Group Exercise #1

While it is possible that during your college education you might be asked to evaluate an object (like a painting in an art history class) or a person (like a political figure in your history class), most of the time in college you will be asked to evaluate ideas. In fact, some people view the essence of a liberal arts education as instilling in the individual the capacity to weigh, consider, and fairly assess concepts and ideas.

How does one go about the process of evaluating ideas? First, of course, a standard of judgment must be worked out. It is impossible to evaluate ideas in the abstract. The standard of judgment gives both a context for evaluation and a method. Second, ideas must have a type of internal consistency or internal logic. If a writer's ideas contradict each other, the odds are that he or she will have a very weak essay. Third, ideas are often judged on the value of their practical application, or on the basis of how much of reality they explain. Ideas that explain a great deal about the world around us and that cover a large number of instances or examples generally are thought superior to ideas that explain very little and only apply to a few select instances.

Keeping these ideas in mind, choose <u>one</u> of the following passages and evaluate the ideas in that passage. Be sure to (1) locate the thesis for that selection; (2) establish standards of judgment for assessing the author's claims; (3) examine the quality of examples, data, and support for the claim (4) evaluate the clarity of language used to express the main ideas, and (5) assess the relevance of the ideas to the intended or actual audience. (Be sure to modify or revise the above criteria and procedures as your group sees fit.) If a selection seems difficult to comprehend, you may wish to summarize the selection as a starting point for your discussion.

a) Stephen W. Hawking, *A Brief History of Time*

The eventual goal of science is to provide a single theory that describes the whole universe. However, the approach most scientists actually follow is to separate the problem into two parts. First, there are the laws that tell us how the universe changes with time. (If we know what the universe is like at any one time, these physical laws tell us how it will look at any later time.) Second, there is the question of the initial state of the universe. Some people feel that science should be concerned with only the first part; they regard the question of the initial situation as a matter for metaphysics or religion. They would say that God, being omnipotent, could have started the universe off any way he wanted. That may be so, but in that case he also could have made it develop in a completely arbitrary way. Yet it appears that he chose to make it evolve in a very regular way according to certain laws. It therefore seems equally reasonable to suppose that there are also laws governing the initial state.

It turns out to be very difficult to devise a theory to describe the universe all in one go. Instead, we break the problem up into bits and invent a number of partial theories. Each of these partial theories describes and predicts a certain limited class of observations, neglecting the effects of other quantities, or representing them by simple sets of numbers. It may be that this approach is completely wrong. If everything in the universe depends on everything else in a fundamental way, it might be impossible to get close to a full solution by investigating parts of the problem in isolation. Nevertheless, it is certainly the way that we have made progress in the past. The classic example again is the Newtonian theory of gravity, which tells us that the gravitational force between two bodies depends only on one number associated with each body, its mass, but otherwise independent of what the bodies are made of. Thus one does not need to have a theory of the structure and constitution of the sun and the planets in order to calculate their orbits.

b) Stanley A. Aronowitz and Henry A. Giroux, *Education Under Siege*

After nearly two decades of benign neglect, schools are once more the subject of an intense national debate. In the recent past, discussion has centered on three issues: whether schools can be the central institution for achieving racial and sexual equality; in higher education, whether the traditional liberal arts curricula are still "relevant" to a changing labor market; and whether the authoritarian classroom stifles the creativity of young children or, conversely, how permissiveness has resulted in a general lowering of educational achievement. All of these issues are still with us, but they have been subsumed under a much larger question: how to make schools adequate to a changing economic, political and ideological environment?

As has been the case with most public issues in American society, the conservatives have seized the initiative and put liberals and progressives on the defensive. Their arguments have force not only because conservatism has become dominant in the ideological realm, but because their critique seems to correspond to the actual situation. In the first place, conservatives have joined radical critics in announcing that the schools have failed to educate, a perception shared by most parents, teachers, and administrators. And, secondly, they have coupled their point with a clear analysis of the causes and a program for curing the affliction. To be sure, their analysis is by no means original or intellectually challenging. They have taken their cue from radical critics who claim that schooling is merely an adjunct to the labor market. But, unlike the left, conservatives criticize the schools for failing to fulfill this function. With some exceptions, they are happy to jettison the traditional intellectual traditions. Instead, they have repeated the 1960s radical attack that schools are not relevant to students' lives. However, at a time when nearly everyone is anxious about his/her place in a rapidly shifting job market, relevance has come to mean little else than job preparation. While many jobs require applicants to know how to read and write and to possess skills for specialized employment, few employers require mastery or even familiarity with literary canon, the arts, and music, much less a secure command of history and the social sciences. Conservatives demand "excellence," by which they usually mean that schools should offer more rigorous science and math curriculum--a notion in keeping with the conservative idea that the mastery of techniques is equivalent to progress. Their language of "achievement," "excellence," "discipline," and "goal orientation" really means vocational education or, in their most traditional mode, a return to the authoritarian classroom armed with the three R's curriculum.

c) Dorothy Leigh Sayers, "Are Women Human?"

The question of "sex equality" is, like all questions affecting human relationships, delicate and complicated. It cannot be settled by loud slogans or hard-and-fast assertions like "a woman is as good as a man" --or "woman's place is in the home" --or "women ought not to take men's jobs." The minute one makes such assertions, one finds one has to qualify them. "A woman is as good as a man" is as meaningless as to say, "a Kaffir is as good as a Frenchman" or "a poet is as good as an engineer" or "an elephant is as good as a racehorse" --it means nothing whatever until you add: "at doing what?" In a religious sense, no doubt, the Kaffir is as valuable in the eyes of god as a Frenchman--but the average Kaffir is probably less skilled in literary criticism than the average Frenchman, and the average Frenchman less skilled than the average Kaffir in tracing the spoor of big game. There might be exceptions on either side: it is largely a matter of heredity and education. When we balance the poet against the engineer, we are faced with a fundamental difference of temperament--so that here our question is complicated by the enormous social problem whether poetry or engineering is "better" for the state, or for humanity in general. There

101

may be people who would like a world that was all engineers or all poets--but most of us would like to have a certain number of each; though here again, we should all differ about the desirable proportion of engineering to poetry. . . . When we come to the elephant and the racehorse, we come down to bed-rock physical differences--the elephant would make a poor showing in the Derby, and the unbeaten Eclipse himself would be speedily eclipsed by an elephant when it came to hauling logs.

That is so obvious that it hardly seems worth saying. But it is the mark of all movements, however well-intentioned, that their pioneers tend, by much lashing of themselves into excitement, to lose sight of the obvious. In reaction against the age-old slogan, "woman is the weaker vessel," or the still more offensive, "woman is a divine creature," we have, I think, allowed ourselves to drift into asserting that "a woman is as good as a man," without always pausing to think what exactly we mean by that. What, I feel, we ought to mean is something so obvious that it is apt to escape attention altogether, viz: not that every woman is, in virtue of her sex, as mentioned; but, that a woman is just as much an ordinary human being as a man, with the same individual preferences, and with just as much right to the tastes and preferences of an individual.

Point/Counterpoint: Considering Alternative Arguments

Choose two of the following questions and write your responses.

1. Mark says to his friend Lee, "I find it difficult to write evaluations. My sense of whether something is good or bad or has any merit or validity at all is very personal and subjective. It's mostly how I feel about something pro or con. How can I put that into words in such a way that people can even understand what I'm saying, much less agree with me?"

How would you respond to Mark's statements?

2. One of the most common aspects of evaluation that you, as a student, would have personal knowledge of is grading. All grading depends upon the development of a standard of judgment. It would be impossible to grade without some sense, some standard of judgment, for what constituted quality, effectiveness, or "good work" in a person's effort or achievement.

Develop what you think would be a good standard of judgment for the evaluation of writing assignments and develop a set of grading criteria that would enable you to apply your standard in the assessment of student papers. If, after you had developed your standard of judgment and your criteria, someone told you that your viewpoint was too limited in perspective and too narrow in application, how would you respond?

3. Evaluate the model and process of evaluation that you have been given by your textbook and your critical thinking journal. Do you agree with this view of evaluation? What aspects would you change, enhance, elaborate upon, or question? Do you have an alternative model that you would propose? How would this model differ from the ones in your texts? In what ways would it be superior to the ones in your texts?

4. One assumption of a critical thinking approach to writing instruction is that thinking skills build upon each other, that the skill of observing details, for example, will complement the skill of description or of investigation, which will, in turn, complement the skill of argumentation and persuasion. Do you agree with this approach? Do you think intellectual skills build upon, influence, and enhance each other? If so, how do you see the skills you have learned in other chapters of your texts, like observing, remembering, etc., fitting in with and enhancing the skill of evaluation? What other intellectual skills do you think evaluation might help in strengthening and developing? Why do you think so?

Summary and Assessment Page

What ideas from Chapter Eight: Evaluating (in either your textbook or your critical thinking journal) helped you the most with your writing? What ideas or techniques did you hope to get from this chapter but did not? What steps do you intend to take to learn those ideas or techniques?

_____

_____

_____

_____

_____

_____

_____

_____

_____

_____

_____

_____

_____

_____

_____

_____

_____

_____

Chapter Nine: Problem Solving

Freewriting #1

What idea/meaning comes to your mind when you think of the term
<u>problem</u>?

_____

_____

_____

_____

_____

_____

Freewriting #2

What critical thinking skills do you think are required for problem solving
or offering solutions to problems?

_____

_____

_____

_____

_____

_____

_____

Problem Solving

As your textbook indicates, problem solving operates on the assumption that you must first be able to prove that a problem exists before you can propose a solution for that problem. This seems a very obvious idea, but you would be amazed at how many students start their papers with the assumption that everyone thinks the same as they do and therefore sees the same problems that they do. Two premises to be aware of here: (1) not everyone agrees that what you think is a problem is a problem; and (2) even if others agree with you that a problem exists, they still might not be seeing the problem or its potential solution from the same angle that you do.

A good idea to remember about problem solving is that defining the problem for your audience is often easier than getting your audience's attention about that problem. Many readers may agree that homelessness is a problem in America, but many may also not want to hear about the depressing statistics associated with "street people." They would prefer to ignore the problem or at least not focus upon it. Capturing the audience's attention, then, will require from you a masterful command of writing techniques, including your ability to observe and describe the problem, remember and narrate specific instances of the problem, and investigate how others have tried to solve the problem before you try to persuade your readers that your solution will work.

Actually, the problems you face in persuading your audience have already been anticipated by Aristotle, a Greek philosopher and rhetorician who saw that arguments, to be effective, must address both the rational and the emotional sides of an audience. The philosophical/rhetorical tradition of Aristotle focused upon rhetoric as "the faculty of observing in any given case the available means of persuasion."

For Aristotle, there were five means of persuasion, three of which were rhetorical, or within the realm of language to persuade. The two non-verbal means involved threat or bribery, while the three verbal means available to the writer or speaker were logos, pathos, and ethos. Essentially, if my act of persuasion (what I want you to do) was for you to get up and close the door for me, I would have five means of persuasion at my disposal. I could threaten you--"Close the door or I'll hit you!" "Close the door or you're grounded for a week and no spending money either." Or, conversely, I could bribe you--"Close the door and I'll give you $5.00." "Close the door and you can borrow my car next weekend."

If these two methods failed, I would be dependent upon verbal means or upon language to get what I wanted. First, I could appeal to your sense of logic or clear reasoning, which Aristotle called logos. "You know, our air conditioning bill for last month was over $150. If you closed the door and kept the cold air from getting out, we might save some on this month's bill." "Close the door so it will be quieter in here and you can get your work done."

If that didn't work, I could appeal to you based on my good character, or ethos. "I've never lied to you, have I? It's very important that you close the door." "Based upon my experience with this neighborhood, I think we will avoid unnecessary gossiping if we keep the door closed."

My last effort would be to appeal to your emotions, which Aristotle called pathos. "Please close the door. You know it's hard for me to get up and down easily these days since I hurt my back." "Please close the door. I had a very hard day at work and I'm exhausted."

In the Rhetoric, Aristotle summed up these three rhetorical means of persuasion very nicely:

> There are, then, these three means of effecting persuasion. The man who is to be in command of them must, it is clear, be able (1) to reason logically [logos], (2) to understand human character and goodness in their various forms [ethos], and (3) to understand the emotions--that is to name them and describe them, to know their causes and the way in which they are excited [pathos].

With ethos, the writer establishes his or her credibility and good character with the audience; with pathos, the writer attempts to appeal to the audience's feelings; and with logos, the speaker uses logical proofs and clear reasoning to make the best case possible for his or her position. As Aristotle perceived it, the most powerful of these means was pathos, since more people are swayed by their emotions than are responsive to logic or ethical appeals.

Exercise #1

Do you agree with Aristotle's view that the strongest of the three rhetorical appeals is pathos, or the appeal to one's emotions? Why might that be? If this is true, and Aristotle is right, how would this influence your view of how to go about writing a problem-solving essay?

_____

_____

_____

_____

_____

_____

_____

_____

_____

_____

_____

_____

_____

_____

_____

_____

_____

_____

_____

_____

Exercise #2

From your textbook, choose either the essay by Neil Postman, "Virtual Students, Digital Classroom" or the essay by John Diebold, "What Are We Waiting For?" Reread the essay you have chosen, looking for examples of Aristotle's three verbal means of persuasion: <u>logos</u>, <u>ethos</u>, and <u>pathos</u>. List two or three specific examples of each type. Which of the types does the author rely on most? Which type does the author use most effectively? Why is that appeal effective for you? (Could you use any of these strategies in the problem-solving essay you are writing?)

_____

_____

_____

_____

_____

_____

_____

_____

_____

_____

_____

_____

_____

_____

_____

_____

_____

_____

Exercise #3

Your textbook gives you a set of techniques to consider (perhaps even follow) in writing a problem-solving essay.

• Identify and understand your audience.

• Demonstrate that a problem exists.

• Propose a solution that will solve the problem.

• Convince your readers your proposal will work.

Evaluate this set of techniques given to you by your textbook. Which of these steps in the problem-solving process do you think is the most complex? Do you think this is an effective model for problem solving, or do you feel there are steps left out? Would you modify this set to include other techniques? What would they be?

_____

_____

_____

_____

_____

_____

_____

_____

_____

_____

_____

_____

_____

_____

Group Exercise #1

For most students, time management is a major problem. Knowing when to study, how to study, how to meet all of one's responsibilities and commitments, and how to handle the rest on one's life while in the midst of going to school and studying represent, for most students, areas in which problem-solving techniques might be of great advantage.

Have the class divide into groups and discuss a problem-solving approach to the issue of time management for students. Let each group identify the issues involved and then propose a set of techniques for time management that might prove valuable. Let the class also critique, respond to, and suggest ways for improving the proposals presented by each group.

Exercise #4

Thinking of writing as an exercise in problem solving and as a problem-solving activity helps us understand that strategies for solving the problem of writing well are extremely important. Without these strategies, writers can flounder and impede themselves at any stage of the process. With these strategies, writers become conscious of their own skills, creativity, and insight and become highly goal-oriented to improve their writing.

Taking a problem-solving perspective toward writing enables a very important shift in one's consciousness to occur, and that is a movement away from viewing writing as a finished, perfect product toward a perception of writing as a series of conscious acts, choices, and decisions that must be performed. If, while you are writing, your whole consciousness is focused upon immediately producing that PERFECT FINISHED ESSAY, you will probably block your writing by terrifying yourself with unreasonable expectations.

If, however, you start to focus instead upon what you want to achieve with your writing and how best you can do that job by tapping into your own creativity, insight, and skills as a writer, then you are involved not with <u>product</u>, but with <u>process</u>. And practice with the <u>process</u> gives you, ironically, a much better chance that your <u>product</u> will be the accomplished piece of writing that you hoped it would be.

What value do you find in viewing writing as a problem-solving activity? Do you agree with this view? Are there, in fact, problems that you face and then solve <u>during</u> your writing process? What strengths and advantages do you find in this perspective? What disadvantages and limitations?

Freewriting #3

Often descriptions of the writing process make it sound like a very simple and straightforward activity. "Choose a topic, decide on your organizational scheme, write your first draft, revise, edit, and turn in your final draft." Do you think that descriptions of the writing process that make it seem so simple and so easy in fact create problems for most writers? Why or why not?

_____

_____

_____

_____

_____

_____

_____

_____

_____

_____

_____

_____

_____

_____

_____

_____

_____

_____

Point/Counterpoint: Considering Alternative Arguments

Choose two of the following questions and write out your responses.

1. A popular saying states that all solutions to problems only create new problems. Do you agree or disagree?

2. Your textbook states, "If the problem is solvable, however, the difficult part is to propose a solution and then persuade others that your solution will, in fact, solve the problem--without creating new problems and without costing too much." One question: If the problem is solvable, wouldn't that mean that a solution was already known? After all, how could you know a problem was solvable if you couldn't already conceptualize its solution? Your thoughts? Do you agree or disagree?

3. After a class on problem-solving techniques, Shannon says to Terry, "I have a problem with this problem solving we are learning. If Aristotle says that pathos is the strongest of the verbal appeals, why am I bothering to study logic and to learn the techniques of well-reasoned arguments?

What would your response be to Shannon's comment?

4. Continuing the conversation, Terry responds, "I think a bigger problem resides with ethos. If people are swayed by the character of a speaker or writer, what's to keep a clever and articulate person from assuming any ethos he or she thinks will work in a given situation? What's to keep anyone from assuming any guise or persona that gets the results he or she wants? Isn't there something strangely disturbing about this, maybe even unethical?"

How would you respond to Terry's views?

_____

_____

_____

_____

_____

_____

Summary and Assessment Page

What ideas from Chapter Nine: Problem Solving (in either your textbook or your critical thinking journal) helped you the most with your writing? What ideas or techniques did you hope to get from this chapter but did not? What steps do you intend to take to learn those ideas or techniques?

_____

_____

_____

_____

_____

_____

_____

_____

_____

_____

_____

_____

_____

_____

_____

_____

_____

_____

Chapter Ten: Arguing

Chapter Ten introduces you to the rhetorical mode of argumentation or persuasion. Argumentation has an aim and purpose different from expressive writing and expository writing. In argumentation, the primary aim is neither to express the writer's feelings (expressive writing) nor to explain a subject (expository writing) but to convince and persuade the writer to accept the writer's point of view or follow the writer's recommendation. Since most writers direct their arguments toward readers who hold either a neutral or an opposing view from the writer's own, persuading the audience toward another point of view represents no small challenge.

In Evaluating and Problem Solving, you were already arguing, trying to convince your reader to accept your judgment of something or to follow your proposal. However in these chapters, you did not necessarily have to consider alternative or opposing arguments. In arguing, however, you must now argue for your side AND against the alternative or opposing claims.

The general structure of an argument is, as Aristotle indicated, "the statement of the case together with its proof." In persuasive writing, the "statement of the case" is called the <u>proposition,</u> (i.e., the claim or thesis) and the proof is called the <u>evidence</u>. All arguments present a thesis or proposition to be argued, together with the evidence that will support that proposition and defend it against challenges from alternative or opposing viewpoints. The proposition (thesis or claim) MUST be for or against something; it cannot take a neutral stance or straddle the fence.

The moment a proposition is framed for an argument, a rudimentary sense of organization is also suggested. To argue for the correctness of viewpoint X and to convince an audience, you would have to: (1) muster sufficient evidence to back up your views and to withstand challenges from the opposition; and (2) anticipate the objections the opposition might raise so that you could counter them at some point in your essay.

This two-point strategy (arguing **for** your claim and **against** the opposition's claim) represents a simplification of the classical argument form. In classical rhetoric, argumentation, or formal persuasion, involved:

• An introduction (<u>Exordium</u>) in which the writer endeavors to capture the reader's attention and to establish some intellectual rapport with the audience.

- A statement of necessary background information (<u>Narratio</u>) relevant to the issue to be argued.

- An exposition (<u>Explicatio</u>) or definition (<u>Definitio</u>) of terms and issues involved in the argument.

- A statement of the proposition to be argued (<u>Partitio</u>).

- A presentation of the forms of evidence to substantiate the proposition (<u>Amplificatio</u>).

- A refutation of alternative or opposing arguments (<u>Refutatio</u>).

- A conclusion (<u>Peroratio</u> or <u>Epilogus</u>), in which the writer makes a strong final appeal to the audience for agreement, action, or change.

This classical form not only identifies the key elements in an argument, but it may be used as an outline, to help you organize your arguments. Some of these elements may be combined or interchanged. For example, some writers define key terms first and then state their main claim; other writers state their claim and then define terms. Some writers prefer to refute alternative arguments before they substantiate their own arguments; some prefer to combine substantiation and refutation, point-by-point as they argue. You should use this list as a guide, not as a point-by-point recipe.

Exercise #1

Explain the purpose of the writing in a typical investigating essay. Then explain the purpose of an explaining or expository essay. How is the purpose of argumentative writing different from informing or explaining? Is it necessary for a writer to inform his or her audience or to explain something to his or her audience in order to write an arguing essay?

_____

_____

_____

_____

_____

_____

_____

_____

_____

_____

_____

_____

_____

_____

_____

_____

_____

_____

_____

Group Exercise #1

Your textbook says that traditional argument is like a <u>debate</u> in which you argue <u>against the opposition</u> and for your claim. Read the following excerpt by Deborah Tannen from her book, *The Argument Culture*. When you finish reading this excerpt, divide into groups of four or five and answer the questions that follow the passage.

Deborah Tannen, from *The Argument Culture*

Balance. Debate. Listening to both sides. Who could question these noble American traditions? Yet today, these principles have been distorted. Without thinking, we have plunged headfirst into what I call the "argument culture."

The argument culture urges us to approach the world and the people in it, in an adversarial frame of mind. It rests on the assumption that opposition is the best way to get anything done. The best way to discuss an idea is to set up a debate; the best way to cover news is to find spokespeople who express the most extreme, polarized views and present them as "both sides"; the best way to settle disputes is litigation that pits one party against the other; the best way to begin an essay is to attack someone; and the best way to show you're really thinking is to criticize.

More and more, our public interactions have become like arguing with a spouse. Conflict can't be avoided in our public lives any more than we can avoid conflict with people we love. One of the great strengths of our society is that we can express these conflicts openly. But just as spouses have to learn ways of settling their differences without inflicting real damage, so we, as a society, have to find constructive ways of resolving disputes and differences.

The war on drugs, the war on cancer, the battle of the sexes, politicians' turf battles--in the argument culture, war metaphors pervade our talk and shape our thinking. . . . Nearly everything is framed as a battle or game in which winning or losing is the main concern. . . .

There are times when it is necessary and right to fight--to defend your country or yourself, to argue for your rights or against offensive or dangerous ideas or actions. What's wrong with the argument culture is the ubiquity, the knee-jerk nature, of approaching any issue, problem or public person in an adversarial way.

Our determination to pursue truth by setting up a fight between two sides leads us to assume that every issue has two sides--no more, no less. . .

How can we overcome our classically American habit of seeing issues in absolutes? We must expand our notion of "debate" to include more dialogue. To do this, we can make special efforts not to think in twos. Mary Catherine Bateson, an anthropologist at Virginia's George Mason University, makes a point of having her class compare three cultures, not two. Then, students are more likely to think about each on its own terms, rather than as opposites.

In the public arena, television and radio producers can try to avoid, whenever possible, structuring public discussions as debates. This means avoiding the format of having two guests discuss an issue. Invite three guests--or one. Perhaps it is time to re-examine the assumption that audiences always prefer a fight.

Instead of asking, "What's the other side?" we might ask, "What are the other sides?" Instead of insisting on hearing both sides," let's insist on hearing "all sides."

We need to find metaphors other than sports and war. Smashing heads does not open minds. We need to use our imaginations and ingenuity to find different ways to seek truth and gain knowledge through intellectual interchange, and add them to our arsenal--or, should I say, to the ingredients for our stew. It will take creativity for each of us to find ways to change the argument culture to a dialogue culture. It's an effort we have to make, because our public and private lives are at stake.

In your groups, discuss the following questions:

1. Tannen says that metaphors involving war, sports, and other conflicts pervade our ways of talking about argument. Make a list of the metaphors in her essay that portray argument as a conflict. Then find the terms or metaphors Tannen uses that suggests argument could be less adversarial. Do you agree with Tannen that these metaphors shape our thinking? Why or why not?

2. In your group, make a list of topics you or your class members are writing about for your arguing essays. Which of these topics would benefit from considering multiple points of view and using dialogue or Rogerian tactics in the argument?   Which topics might best be covered in a traditional, adversarial, pro-con form of argument?

3. This critical thinking workbook invites you to challenge assumptions. At the end of every chapter, there is a "Point/Counterpoint: Considering Alternative Arguments" section.   This section used to be called "Point/Counterpoint: Considering Opposing Arguments." Should the name have been changed from "opposing" to "alternative?" Also, does the phrase "point/counterpoint" limit our critical thinking by only inviting us to think in pairs, in twos, or in "pros" and "cons?"   Or does it sharpen your thinking to imagine opposing points of view?

Group Exercise #2

Errors in reasoning are known as <u>fallacies</u>. Being aware of potential fallacies or errors in logic will not only make your own writing clearer, but it also will help you analyze and refute alternative arguments as you write your own arguing essay.

For this group activity, members should bring to class examples from the print media of essays, letters to the editor, ads, campaign literature, bumper stickers, etc., in which logical fallacies play a large role in influencing audience response. Based on their sample, groups should determine which of the logical fallacies (see below list) appear <u>most frequently</u> in their examples. Groups should then identify the one or two ads or editorials displaying the greatest <u>number</u> of logical fallacies. They should prepare to share their analyses with the rest of the class.

To help you identify logical fallacies in the print media examples, review the list of fallacies in your textbook and then read the following alphabetical list.

- <u>Ad hoc</u>, in which because X and Y occur together, X is assumed to have caused Y. "I played my best round of golf wearing a plaid shirt; I'm going to wear a plaid shirt the next time I play." In our everyday lives, much of the power attributed to "lucky charms" is the result of <u>ad hoc</u> reasoning. Just because a student performed well on a biology exam while he was carrying a rabbit's foot in his pocket is no guarantee that the rabbit's foot had anything to do with the student's good grade. [See also <u>post hoc</u>.]

- <u>Ad hominem</u>, in which the character of the speaker, rather than the quality of his or her argument, is attacked. "Don't listen to John's views on economics; he's a Socialist."

- <u>Ad populem</u>, in which an argument is formulated upon an appeal to popular prejudices and biases. "Don't listen to John's views on family life; he's a homosexual."

- <u>The Bandwagon</u>, which assumes that something is correct because "everybody" is doing it. "YellowBlockers sunglasses are excellent; everybody's wearing them today."

- <u>Begging the question</u>, in which an assumption is taken for granted that needs to be established by proof. "Don't trust John on investments;

he's a liar" --rather than establishing that John is lying in this particular instance.

- Circular argument, in which a statement simply restates rather than proves its claim. "Women make wonderful mothers because they have motherly instincts."

- Either/Or, in which a complex issue is reduced to only two alternatives. "Either we eliminate drug use in our high schools or American education is doomed."

- False analogy, in which there are not enough important similarities between two subjects being compared to warrant the conclusions being drawn. "Political radicals are just like psychopaths; they both think the system is unjust and unfair."

- False cause, in which a complex issue that is the result of many causes is explained in terms of only one cause. "The decline of the American family can be attributed directly to the Women's Liberation movement." [See also hasty generalization.]

- Genetic fallacy, in which the class that a person is from, and not the person's own qualities or qualifications, becomes the standard of judgment. "You can't possibly trust Howard; he's a lawyer."

- Hasty generalization, in which the sample is too small for logical conclusions to be drawn. "All athletes are bad in math; my friends, Joe and Carol, are on the swim team, and they can't even pass algebra."

- Hidden generalization, in which one premise or assumption is left out or excluded from the argument. "Bob graduated from Harvard, so his family must have political connections." The hidden assumption or premise here is that all people who graduate from Harvard come from families of wealth and political power.

- Post hoc, which assumes that because one thing chronologically follows another that it therefore causes it. Post hoc comes from post hoc ergo propter hoc, meaning "after this, therefore because of this." Imagine that in the afternoon, you unknowingly eat some contaminated oysters. Three hours later, for dinner, you have cantaloupe with your dinner. Later that evening, you become violently ill. Recently, you read an article in the paper about melons contaminated with salmonella, so you conclude (having forgotten about the oysters) that the melons are the cause of your illness. To avoid a <u>post hoc</u> fallacy, you should not assume the cause of your illness is the most recent suspicious thing you ate.

- <u>Red herring</u>, in which the audience is diverted from the real issue by an irrelevant fact or argument. Urged to install pollution controls in its factories, a company might argue that the increased cost of the pollution controls will necessitate job layoffs, a result that nobody would want. Instead of focusing upon the issue of pollution control, the company may use the red herring of job layoffs to divert attention from the real health issue.

- <u>Rigged question</u>, in which the writer poses a question in such a way that any answer requires an admission of guilt. "Have you stopped cheating on your income taxes?" Even the answer "Yes" implies that you have cheated, and "No" implies that you are still cheating on your taxes. [See also <u>begging the question</u>.]

- <u>Slanting</u>, in which language or data are represented in terms that encourage the reader to accept a distorted or biased view of the subject. To argue, for example, that the fact that 30% of all marriages fail is proof that marriage is a declining societal institution overlooks the fact that 70% of all marriages do not fail.

- <u>Slippery slope</u>, in which one aspect of an argument is pushed to an extreme and illogical conclusion. "If a person smokes marijuana, the next step is cocaine, then heroin, then the total collapse of that person's moral character."

- <u>Unrepresentative sample</u>, in which the samples used are not representative of the whole group. "92% of all women surveyed oppose abortion" is an unrepresentative sample if the only women surveyed were members of a fundamentalist religious group.

In addition to fallacies involving abuses of reason, there are also a number of <u>psychological</u> fallacies that play upon the feelings of the audience. Both the <u>ad hominem</u> and <u>ad populem</u> fallacies also belong to this category. Rhetoric recognizes the legitimate role of pathos, or appeals to the emotions or feelings of an audience, but psychological fallacies conceal or distort the real issues at hand in an attempt to unfairly manipulate readers.

- <u>Appeal to pity</u>, in which an extraneous appeal is used to draw unwarranted pity and sympathy from an audience. "I shouldn't have to fail my math class; my dog had died just the day before I took the test."

- <u>Appeal to force</u>, in which one's social, political, or economic power over an individual gives unwarranted weight to one's argument or line of reasoning. "Don's proposal for a merger of our company with Holcraft Industries is an excellent one; if you don't vote for it, you may not be promoted to assistant manager and you might lose your job entirely." Often examples of sexual harassment in the workplace illustrate an appeal to force.

- <u>Appeal to ceremony</u>, in which the locale and formality are assumed to give truth and importance to data and/or conclusions. When TV ads present information on the latest cold medicines, the odds are that the speaker in the ad will be wearing a white lab coat and/or standing in front of a nurse's or doctor's station on a hospital floor. The presence of such props lends false credence to the information. The cold medicine will be good or bad, and the test results will substantiate or negate this fact, whether the spokesperson is dressed in a white lab coat or not or speaks to you from a formal lectern or merely chats in a coffee lounge.

- <u>Appeal to tradition</u>, which assumes that since something has always been done a certain way therefore that way has intrinsic merit and is superior than other methods. "We cannot change to an automated system of registration; we've been registering students for their classes without data processing for over eighty years, and there's no need to change the system now."

- <u>Appeal to ignorance</u>, which assumes that a proposition that cannot be proven false must therefore be true. "No one can prove that God doesn't exist, so God must exist."

- <u>Appeal to humor</u>, in which humor is used to denigrate an opponent or trivialize his or her views. "We all know why Congresswoman Blake is opposed to an economic ban on South Africa; South Africa is a leading exporter of diamonds, and we all know how women love their diamonds."

Group Exercise #3

The class should review the types of claims, the logical appeals (logos, ethos, and pathos) and the list of logical fallacies in the textbook. Then the class should divide into groups, and each group should design an advertising campaign, a political campaign, or a political action movement that uses a substantial number of the logical fallacies in its appeals. After each group has presented its ideas, the class will discuss the rhetorical strategies used by each group and evaluate the types of impact such strategies might have upon an audience.

Exercise #2

This exercise provides you with an opportunity to interpret a passage, state a proposition or claim, and defend your thesis through logical reasoning.   The process itself is similar to taking an essay examination in that the interpretation of this passage depends more upon your critical thinking skills and rhetorical resources than it does upon heavily researched evidence. Read the passage and make your best case for whatever point of view you adopt.

Here is a very familiar parable, the parable of the prodigal son (Luke 15: 11-32):

A man had two sons. When the younger told his father, "I want my share of your estate now, instead of waiting until you die!" his father agreed to divide his wealth between his sons.

A few days later this younger son packed all his belongings and took a trip to a distant land, and there wasted all his money on parties and prostitutes. About the time his money was gone a great famine swept over the land, and he began to starve. He persuaded a local farmer to hire him to feed his pigs. The boy became so hungry that even the pods he was feeding the swine looked good to him. And no one gave him anything.

When he finally came to his senses, he said to himself, "At home even the hired men have food enough and to spare, and here I am dying of hunger! I will go home to my father and say, "Father, I have sinned against both heaven and you, and am no longer worthy of being called your son. Please take me on as a hired man."

So he returned home to his father. And while he was still a long distance away, his father saw him coming and was filled with loving pity and ran and embraced him and kissed him.

His son said to him, "Father, I have sinned against heaven and you, and am not worthy of being called your son."

But his father said to the slaves, "Quick! Bring the finest robe in the house and put it on him. And a jeweled ring for his finger; and shoes. And kill the calf we have in the fattening pen. We must celebrate with a feast, for this son of mine was dead and has returned to life. He was lost and is found." So the party began.

128

Meanwhile, the older son was in the fields working; when he returned home, he heard dance music coming from the house, and he asked one of the servants what was going on.

"Your brother is back," he was told, "and your father has killed the calf we were fattening and has prepared a great feast to celebrate his coming home again unharmed."

The older brother was angry and wouldn't go in. His father came out and begged him, but he replied, "All these years I've worked hard for you and never once refused to do a single thing you told me to; and in all that time you never gave me even one young goat for a feast with my friends. Yet when this son of yours comes back after spending your money on prostitutes, you celebrate by killing the finest calf we have on the place.

"Look, dear son," his father said to him, "you and I are very close, and everything I have is yours. But it is right to celebrate. For he is your brother; and he was dead and has come back to life! He was lost and is found!"

Your assignment for this exercise is to address this question: Does the older brother have a case? Write the best argument he could make for his point of view.

Then write how the father might respond to this argument.

_____

_____

_____

_____

_____

_____

_____

_____

_____

Freewriting #1

Interpreting what you think is the central concern of the parable of the prodigal son (such as love, forgiveness, etc.) is a preliminary stage to addressing the issue of whether a case can be made for the elder son's position. Discuss what you consider to be the central concern of the parable and how your interpretation influenced the argument you developed.

Exercise #3

Apply your skills in interpretation to the following passage, which is a Chinese parable. What inferences can be drawn from this parable? How can those inferences be formulated into claims or thesis statements for an argumentation essay?

On a certain street in a Chinese city there was a poor beggar who held out his cup all day begging for rice or whatever the passersby chose to give him.

One day the beggar saw a great parade coming down his street headed by the Emperor riding in his stately rickshaw and freely handing out gifts to his subjects. The poor beggar was filled with delight.

"Now," thought Woo, "my great opportunity has come. For once I shall receive a worthy gift," and he danced with joy.

When the Emperor reached him, Woo held out his cup with great earnestness, but instead of the expected gift from the Emperor his majesty asked Woo for a gift.

Poor Woo was greatly disappointed and vexed; so he reached in his cup and with much grumbling handed the Emperor two of the smallest grains of rice he could find. The Emperor passed on.

All that day Woo fumed and grumbled. He denounced the Emperor, he berated Buddha, he was cross to those who spoke to him, and few people even stopped to speak to him or drop grains of rice in his cup.

That night when Woo reached his poor hut and poured out his scant supply of rice, he found in his cup two nuggets of gold just the size of the grains of rice he had given to the Emperor.

_____

_____

_____

_____

_____

131

Group Exercise #4

An important part of writing effective arguing essays is refuting counterarguments. Addressing the alternative or opposing arguments gives weight and merit to arguing essays by indicating that the author has carefully thought out the implications of his or her views. If handled diplomatically, responding to opposing arguments will help persuade your audience.

In refuting counterarguments, you have the following options:
You can attack their <u>evidence</u>, their <u>claims or recommendations</u>, or their <u>logic</u>.

- **Evidence:** Does the opposition have <u>sufficient</u> or <u>valid</u> evidence? Does their evidence come from <u>reliable</u> sources? Is their data old or out of date? What <u>new evidence</u> might alter their claims?

- **Claims:** Are their claims <u>practical</u> or realistic? What are the possible <u>drawbacks</u> or disadvantages if their ideas are accepted or implemented? Will their ideas work in the <u>long term</u> as well as the short term? Are they addressing root causes or only the <u>symptoms</u> of the problem?

- **Logic:** Examine the <u>relationship</u> between the opposition's evidence and their claims. Do their claims follow logically from their evidence? Do they have any <u>logical fallacies</u> in their argument? Do they make any <u>hasty generalizations</u> or have any <u>false assumptions</u> about the issue?

Point/Counterpoint: Considering Alternative Arguments

Choose two of the following questions and write out your responses.

1. The first freewriting presented to you in Chapter Nine of your textbook is to argue either for or against the following claim: "High schools today are a waste of time."   Argue for or against the claim that this <u>topic</u> is a waste of time.

2. Consider the Rogerian model for argumentation and Deborah Tannen's remarks in the excerpt from *The Argument Culture*. Can persuasion really occur in a friendly atmosphere? Are there times when argument must be confrontational? Do you think that dialogue, mediation, or a Rogerian approach is naive, perhaps even possibly misguided? Can you think of situations in which such an empathetic view of one's opposition could work against the success of the point one was making with an audience?

3. Two assumptions underlie most views of argumentation: (1) that a reasoned, intellectual approach is the best (or at least preferred) method to take and is the most effective in winning over an audience; and (2) that the majority of arguments can be solved or resolved through reasoned discourse and an exchange of ideas that then become open to scrutiny and question. Do you agree with these assumptions? Why or why not? Are there other assumptions you would propose as more valid? What might those be?

4. A fellow classmate tells you that the study of argumentation has given him great hope. Alternative or opposing viewpoints can be presented, discussed, and reconciled, and, in this way, truth can be arrived at. What would be your response to your classmate? Do you agree with his views? Do you think truth can be arrived at via argumentation? What would be your definition of truth in terms of argumentation? How would an audience know when and how that truth had been arrived at?

_____

_____

_____

_____

Summary and Assessment Page

What ideas from Chapter Ten: Arguing (in either your textbook or your critical thinking journal) helped you the most with your writing? What ideas or techniques did you hope to get from this chapter but did not? What steps do you intend to take to learn those ideas or techniques?

_____

_____

_____

_____

_____

_____

_____

_____

_____

_____

_____

_____

_____

_____

_____

_____

_____

_____

_____

Chapter Eleven: Responding to Literature

At the beginning of your textbook's chapter on Responding to Literature, the following quotation appears:

No one else can
read a literary work for us.
The benefits of literature can emerge
only from creative activity on
the part of the reader.

--Louise Rosenblatt

This statement contains several assumptions that you should be aware of before you read the short stories contained in this chapter. First, it suggests that a literary work does not exist solely on the page, but it is the result of a joint creation or collaboration on the part of the writer and the reader. The author has written the words, but the reader must give them context, imagination, life, and meaning. Second, it implies that there is not one reading or interpretation of the story that is THE ANSWER. Although readers may agree about some general guidelines for interpreting a particular story, no one else can--or should--read the story for us. Finally, it suggests that reading literature is a creative activity, that reading is not a passive but an active, imaginative, and creative act. Exercising your own creativity--not just analyzing characters names or plot elements--is an important goal of literary study.

In your study of literature, therefore, be prepared to read as carefully and creatively as possible, but don't assume that you should "get" one particular interpretation that is the "right" one. Instead, be prepared to share your interpretations with your classmates. Be prepared to hear other's interpretations and adjust your own understanding as you learn more. Learn to reread a poem or short story in light of the evidence or interpretations that your classmates and your teacher find. Appreciating and understanding literature is an ongoing process, not a single act or event.

Freewriting #1

Choose a short story or a poem that you read recently or that you studied in a previous English class. Who was the author and what was the title? If possible, find a copy of the poem or story and reread it. Below, write for five minutes on what that literary work meant to you. What did you find most interesting about it? How did you interpret its meaning?

_____

_____

_____

_____

_____

_____

_____

_____

_____

_____

_____

_____

_____

_____

_____

_____

_____

_____

_____

Exercise #1

Read the first short story, "The Story of an Hour," by Kate Chopin. In the space below, explain how your reading of that story illustrates or does not illustrate the validity of Louise Rosenblatt's chapter opening quotation. Was your reading a "joint creation" by both the author and yourself? Second, was your interpretation of the story in any way unique or personal? Finally, was there any sense in which your reading and interpretation was creative? Explain.

_____

_____

_____

_____

_____

_____

_____

_____

_____

_____

_____

_____

_____

_____

_____

_____

_____

_____

Interpreting literature often contains a bit of riddle solving. All children, we know, love puzzles and riddles, but even as adults, we often enjoy a riddle that teases our imagination. Probably the most famous literary example is the Riddle of the Sphinx. In "Oedipus Rex," Sophocles has Oedipus solve the Sphinx's riddle: "What walks on four legs in the morning, two legs at noon, and three legs in the evening?" The answer, of course, is man, who crawls as a child, walks upright in youth and middle age, and walks with a cane in the old age. In the context of the play, however, the riddle is more than a single, simple answer: The answer is both man and Oedipus himself, for the riddle actually foreshadows Oedipus' life. At the end of the play Oedipus blinds himself because he cannot solve the riddle of his own life, and he must tap his way out of the city using a cane.

Below are some Old English riddles, poems written about a particular thing or animal. Read each of the poems and see if you can guess the riddle from the poet's clues. As you read, however, remember that there may be more than one "correct" answer:

My attire is noiseless   when I tread the earth,
Rest in its dwellings   or ride its waters.
At times my pinions   and the lofty air
Lift me high   o'er the homes of men,
And the strength of the clouds   carries me far
High over the folk.   My feathers gay
Sound and make music,   singing shrill,
When no longer I linger   by field or flood,
But soar in air,   a wandering spirit.

My house is not quiet,   I am not loud;
But for us God fashioned   our fate together.
I am the swifter,   at times the stronger,
My house more enduring,   longer to last.
At times I rest;   my dwelling still runs;
Within it I lodge   as long as I live.
Should we two be severed,   my death is sure.

Oft I must strive   with wind and wave,
Battle them both   when under the sea
I feel out the bottom,   a foreign land.
In lying still   I am strong in the strife;
If I fail in that   they are stronger than I
And, wrenching me loose,   soon put me to rout.
They wish to capture   what I must keep.
I can master them both   if my grip holds out,
If the rocks bring succor   and lend support,
Strength in the struggle.   Ask me my name!

Exercise #3

Sometimes riddles are built into a plot, adding to the suspense and intrigue of the story. At the heart of the following poem, "Sir Patrick Spence," is a riddle about what actually happened. The following anonymous folk ballad is written in an archaic Scots dialect with some unfamiliar spellings, but with a bit of work, you can piece together the outlines of this tragic story.

Read the poem, and then explain <u>what</u> happens, <u>what might</u> have happened, what the <u>riddles</u> in the story are, and what you think the story means.

Sir Patrick Spense

The king sits in Dumferling toune,
    Drinking the blude-reid wine;
"O whar will I get guid° sailor,   °good
    To sail this schip of mine?"

Up and spak an eldern knicht,
    Sat at the kings richt° kne: °right
"Sir Patrick Spence is the best sailor,
    That sails upon the se.°"   °sea

The king has written a braid° letter,   °open
    And signed it wi' his hand,
And sent it to Sir Patrick Spence,
    Was walking on the sand.

The first line that Sir Patrick red,
    A loud lauch° lauched he;   °laugh
The next line that Sir Patrick red,
    The teir blinded his ee.

"O wha° is this has done this deid,   °who
    This ill deid don to me,
To send me out this time o' the yeir,
    To sail upon the se?

"Mak hast, mak hast, my mirry men all,
    Our guid schip sails the morne":
"O say na sae, my master deir,
    For I feir a deadlie storme.

"Late late yestreen I saw the new moone,
    Wi' the auld moone in hir arme,
And I feir, I feir, my deir master,
    That we will cum to harme."

O our Scots nobles wer richt laith°   °loath
    To weet their cork-heild schoone;°   °cork-heeled shoes
Bot lang owre° a' the play wer playd,   °before
    Thair hats they swam aboone.°   °above (the water)

O lang, lang may their ladies sit,
    Wi' thair fans into their hand,
Or eir° they se Sir Patrick Spence   °before
    Cum sailing to the land.

O lang, lang may the ladies stand,
    Wi' thair gold kems in their hair,
Waiting for their ain deir lords,
    For they'll se thame na mair.

Have owre,° have owre to Aberdour,   °over
    It's fiftie fadom° deip,   °fathoms
And thair lies guid Sir Patrick Spence,
    Wi' the Scots lords at his feit.

_____

_____

_____

_____

_____

_____

Group Exercise #1

Your instructor will bring one of the following poems to class to study in groups: Emily Dickinson, "Because I could not stop for Death," Robert Frost, "Stopping by Woods," William Shakespeare's Sonnet 73 (That time of year thou mayst in me behold), or William Blake, "The Lamb" and "The Tyger."

Your group should read each poem aloud, several times. After each reading, your group should discuss what they think the "riddle" in the poem is--and what their possible "answers" to the riddle might be. A recorder in each group should take notes and should prepare to report to the rest of the class what guesses about the riddle or the meaning the group came up with and what the consensus interpretation of the poem was.

Group Exercise #2

In your group, discuss the possible "riddles" contained in Kate Chopin's "Story of an Hour" or in Eudora Welty's "A Worn Path." Look particularly at characters, actions, and images that contain ambiguity or that might suggest more than one possible interpretation. In your group, find as many of these cruxes or riddles as you can. How does your group's interpretation at each of these points affect your overall interpretation of the story?

Point/Counterpoint: Considering Alternative Arguments

Choose two of the following questions and write out your responses.

1. Your text says, "A story is like an empty balloon that we must inflate with the warm breath of our imagination and experience.   Our participation makes us partners with the authors in the artistic creation." What can this statement possibly mean?   Do you agree that you are a "partner" in creating the story, or did Kate Chopin really write her story and you are just reading it?

2.   After class, Roberto says, "I don't get it.   We're supposed to give evidence to support our interpretation, but we can't give a plot summary or retell the events of the story. So how are we supposed to write our essay?" Explain how you would answer his question.

3.   Your critical thinking journal says that there is no one RIGHT ANSWER that is the correct interpretation of the story.   Do you agree with this statement? Aren't there some wrong answers or interpretations of the story? How can there be several right answers?

4.   Your text says that responding to literature requires sharing ideas among your class members or among members of a group. Isn't it possible to read a short story and understand it all by yourself? Can't you read a poem and interpret it by reading it to yourself? Do you have to discuss it in order to have a satisfactory interpretation all by yourself?

_____

_____

_____

_____

_____

_____

_____

_____

Summary and Assessment Page

What ideas from Chapter Eleven: Responding to Literature (in either your textbook or your critical thinking journal) helped you the most with your writing? What ideas or techniques did you hope to get from this chapter but did not? What steps do you intend to take to learn those ideas or techniques?

_____

_____

_____

_____

_____

_____

_____

_____

_____

_____

_____

_____

_____

_____

_____

_____

_____

_____

_____

_____

Chapter Twelve: Writing a Research Paper

Freewriting #1

What does the concept of writing a research paper mean to you? What ideas (or memories) come to mind?

_____

_____

_____

_____

_____

_____

_____

_____

_____

_____

_____

_____

_____

_____

_____

_____

_____

_____

_____

Freewriting #2

What type of audience do you think a research paper is aimed at? Why do you think so? What values underlie your assumptions? What line of reasoning leads you to your conclusions?

_____

_____

_____

_____

_____

_____

_____

_____

_____

_____

_____

_____

_____

_____

_____

_____

_____

_____

_____

Writing a Research Paper

A research paper helps us address the question of why. It responds to and addresses our curiosity about a given subject, helping us extend our range of knowledge beyond what we already know into the area of what we can find out and discover.

Interestingly, though, most people's view of a research paper is very negative. They perceive writing a research paper as one of the more drab and unexciting experiences they can imagine. Perhaps they were overzealously hounded by instructors who told them the essence of good research was the 3 x 5 note card. Perhaps they recall volumes and volumes of journal articles and books they had to read and felt they never could assimilate. Perhaps the idea of confronting volumes of published research made them feel intellectually inadequate and made them believe they had little to contribute to the subject.

Basically, though, writing a research paper has a simple ultimate goal, a goal you have already practiced in your previous papers. A research paper requires four critical thinking activities: identifying and defining a issue or problem, finding out what others have said and written about this topic, proposing solutions to this problem, and communicating your findings to a general or specialized audience. The research paper allows you opportunities to improve your skills in all four areas.

Writing a research paper allows you to draw on your skills you have practiced in previous section of your course, your textbook, and your critical thinking journal. The skills you learned in keeping your journal will prove essential in keeping your research log. The skills you learned in observing, remembering, and investigating will be essential. Finally, your skill in narrowing the scope of your essay and finding an angle or focus appropriate for your audience will be more important for this essay than for almost any other essay you have written.

Group Exercise #1

Class members should organize into groups of four or five and then discuss plagiarism. A group recorder should take notes for the group as it focuses on <u>defining</u> plagiarism.

Groups should consider if plagiarism can occur even if the writer does not intend to cheat. Groups should consider if plagiarism occurs if a source is accurately cited but the passage in question is a word-for-word transcription without quotation marks. Finally, groups should devise a policy to be used in this class for papers that exhibit plagiarism. For illustration purposes, your instructor may hand out a sample research paper that has documentation problems that suggest plagiarism has occurred.

After answering each of these questions, groups should be prepared to report their findings to the rest of the class.

Group Exercise #2

In groups of four or five, practice narrowing and focusing at least three of the following general topics. **Narrowing** a subject means dividing the subject into smaller parts and selecting one aspect for your topic. **Focusing** a topic means finding some personal experience, an angle, problem, or special conflict that might interest your intended audience.

Read and discuss the following sample, and then discuss how to narrow and focus each of the numbered topics. A group recorder should write down the group's ideas for narrowing and focusing each of the topics.

Sample: Cancer

Narrowing: Use the "Wh" questions to help narrow the subject.

Who   Select <u>one group</u> affected by cancer: infants, children, women, men, native Americans, African Americans, whites, Europeans, Australians, French, etc.

What   Select <u>one kind</u> of skin cancer: colon cancer, breast cancer, etc.

When   Select <u>one time period</u> important in the study of cancer: cancer treatment in ancient Greece, cancer diagnosis in 18th century Germany, cancer research in the U. S. during the 1980s, etc.

Where   Select <u>one geographical area</u>: cancers prevalent in nuclear test site communities in New Mexico and Arizona; cancers resulting from Love Canal pollution; cancers occurring in New Orleans, Los Angeles, Detroit, or St. Louis. If possible, see how this issue has <u>local</u> implications.

Why   Select <u>one particular cause</u> of cancer: cancers caused by smoking, cancers caused by ultraviolet radiation, cancers caused by inhaling asbestos, cancers caused by PCBs, etc.

How   Select <u>one particular treatment</u> (how cancer is cured): chemotherapy, radiation, surgery, diet, etc.

Focusing: Look for some personal experience, an angle, a particular problem, or a special conflict that might interest you or your audience.

Personal Experience   Draw on your own personal experience.   How might your experiences give you a way to focus your topic?   Have you or any of your family or friends been afflicted with cancer?

Angle   Look for a particular or original point-of-view on your subject: how children treat their peers who have cancer; how husbands or wives cope with a spouse who has cancer; how cancer research is funded by generous donations from corporate America; how cancer gives patients and and their friends inner strength; how laughter therapy is used to help heal cancer patients; and etc.

Problem   Look for a problem that scientists, individuals, or drug companies are trying to solve: How genetic engineering contributes to cancer treatment;   What the biotech companies are contributing to cancer treatment; How special drugs allow chemotherapy to kill cancer cells without debilitating the patient;   How a national health program should cover cancer, etc.

Conflict   Look for difficult questions, conflicting claims, or paradoxes in the field: How can terminal cancer patients and their families decide when to continue treatment and when to terminate life? If hundreds of food substances can cause cancer in rats, how does the consumer know what he or she can safely eat?   Can the highly costly but necessary treatment of cancer continue without bankrupting individuals or the society?

Practice Narrowing and Focusing These Subjects:

1. Environment
2. Political elections
3. Racism and sexism
4. Dieting
5. College athletics
6. Computer technology
7. Sexually transmitted diseases
8. Aging
9. Advertising
10. New cars

Exercise #1

Select a topic from Group Exercise #2 and then write out a set of questions in an interview designed to elicit information about that topic. First, specify the person and his or her profession that you would be interviewing. Explain why that person would be useful for your topic. Write out your goals or aims of the questions you intend to ask: How would your intended questions help you (1) learn additional information about your subject; (2) discover how to narrow or focus your topic; (3) uncover additional sources for your paper?

Write out your questions below:

_____

_____

_____

_____

_____

_____

_____

_____

_____

_____

_____

_____

_____

_____

_____

Group Exercise #3

Let the class divide into groups. Each group is responsible for visiting the library and writing a user's guide to a particular section or aspect of the library's offerings or holdings. Some possible topics for investigating and reporting: how to use the computer on-line card catalog; how to use science and technology indexes; how to locate and find government documents; how to use interlibrary loan; or how to photocopy articles on microfilm.

Let each group present its user's guide and have it critiqued for clarity by the class as a whole. When the presentations are completed, groups should revise and distribute their guides to the rest of the class.

Point/Counterpoint: Considering Alternative Arguments

Choose two of the following questions and write out your responses.

1. Has reading Chapter Twelve on research papers in both your textbook and your workbook changed any of your initial views of research papers that you expressed in Freewritings #1 and #2? If so, what views have changed and why?

2. Melissa has completed her workbook exercises on the research paper. She turns to you and says, "No matter what this book and my textbook say, I still think writing a research paper is an artificial exercise. It's too contrived, too formulaic, and too uninteresting to me."

How would you respond to Melissa's comments?

3. Virginia agrees with Melissa. "It is not the natural way that people write. And beside, have you ever read an interesting research paper? If research papers are supposed to be such a big deal and teach us so much about writing, why are they all so boring?"

How would you respond to Virginia's views?

4. Phillip responds to Virginia by saying, "I don't like research papers because they rob me of my personal voice. I don't want to write and sound like a textbook or a journal article. I want to sound like me. Besides, I think it's ironic that the textbook and the critical thinking journal have spent so much time emphasizing the personal voice in writing and how important it is, and then take away that voice for these research papers? It all seems an unfair contradiction to me."

How would you respond to Phillip?

5. Martin says, "The problem for me is that I like the kind of writing that shakes up the world and makes people open their eyes and think. I don't think research papers do that. If anything, they seem, to me, like dreary exercises in a lot of busywork associated with library searches and making out 3 x 5 note cards. Who cares about this type of writing, and what practical effect does it have on any one?"

How would you respond to Martin's views?

Summary and Assessment Page

What ideas from Chapter Twelve: Writing a Research Paper (in either your textbook or your critical thinking journal) helped you the most with your writing? What ideas or techniques did you hope to get from this chapter but did not? What steps do you intend to take to learn those ideas or techniques?

_____

_____

_____

_____

_____

_____

_____

_____

_____

_____

_____

_____

_____

_____

_____

_____

_____

_____

_____

_____